'NICE WHEN THEY ARE YOUNG':
CONTEMPORARY CHRISTIANITY IN FAMILIES AND SCHOOLS

To Catriona, Tom and Fiona

'Nice when they are young': Contemporary Christianity in families and schools

MAIRI LEVITT
Centre for Professional Ethics
University of Central Lancashire

Avebury

Aldershot · Brookfield USA · Hong Kong · Singapore · Sydney

Published by
Avebury
Ashgate Publishing Ltd
Gower House
Croft Road
Aldershot
Hants GU11 3HR
England

Ashgate Publishing Company
Old Post Road
Brookfield
Vermont 05036
USA

BV
1475.2
.L45
1996

British Library Cataloguing in Publication Data

Levitt, Mairi
    'Nice when they are young' : contemporary Christianity in
    families and schools
    1. Christian education - Great Britain
    I. Title
    207.4 ' 1

    ISBN 1 85972 388 8

Library of Congress Catalog Card Number: 96-85192

Printed and bound by Athenaeum Press, Ltd.,
Gateshead, Tyne & Wear.

Contents

Figures and Tables

Acknowledgements

I would like to thank all those in 'Penvollard' who took part in this study; the headteachers who allowed their schools to take part, the teachers, clergy and mothers who were interviewed and the children who grew from childhood to young adulthood in the course of the research. For awakening my interest in sociology of religion when at Edinburgh University I would like to thank Professor Robin Gill who is now at the University of Kent at Canterbury and for help and encouragement with the research for this book, I am grateful to Dr Grace Davie at Exeter University. I would like to thank Kerry Wilding for her invaluable help in preparing the manuscript and the Centre for Professional Ethics for giving me the time to complete it. Finally, thank you to my parents and Rev. Nigel Stimpson for proof reading skills.

The photographs on pages 73 and 74 are reproduced by kind permission of John Rapston from his collection. Those on pages 72 and 75 were taken by David Hambly and reproduced with his permission.

Mairi Levitt
March 1996

Introduction

> It is very important for children...there's a certain magic for a child in religion ....
> I liked mine to go when they were younger (mothers in Penvollard study)

The core of this book is a study of one area in Cornwall, here named 'Penvollard', and the attitudes and beliefs of a group of families living there who had a child age 10 or 11, in the final year of a local primary school when the study began. All the families were Christian or nominally Christian, not through special selection but reflecting the local population. One impetus to studying the nominally Christian was the building of a new and attractive church aided school in another Cornish town where I lived. There were already many small village aided schools but the diocesan policy was to provide the choice of a church school education by building schools in the expanding towns, where alternative schools already existed. Parents already had a choice of three schools but such was their enthusiasm for the new church school that children were put on the waiting list at birth and were only prevented by the head teacher from putting them down before birth by the fact that they could not give the baby's sex! Despite the desirability of obtaining the Vicar's signature for the application form the intake seemed to be socially rather than religiously 'skewed'. I now know that their enthusiasm was not unusual.

The second impetus to begin the study was the intriguing finding by Leslie Francis that Church of England aided schools had a negative effect, or at best no influence, on children's attitudes towards Christianity, once other factors such as parental attendance at a church, gender, social class and locality were taken into account (Francis 1989). In contrast Francis found Roman Catholic schools to have a positive effect. So Anglican church schools are popular but they do not make children more positive towards Christianity. Whether parents actually value church schools

1

because they expect them to influence their children's religious attitudes is another issue.

Two areas of investigation followed from these beginnings: Anglican schools, their aims and achievements, and the beliefs and attitudes of the parents who choose them in preference to a county school. Since around a quarter of children attend an aided primary school (mainly Roman Catholic or Anglican) but less than 10 per cent of the adult population of England attend a church regularly there must be many children from non-religious and nominally Christian homes in these schools, as well as children with other faith backgrounds. I was particularly interested in those who would claim some sort of Christian affiliation and/or belief but could not be said to be active members of any church. For this reason I chose a small Cornish town in which to base the research, a town with a population that was at least nominally Christian.

I decided to follow a group of children from their primary school to the comprehensive school and study their religious attitudes and that of their mothers while also gathering information on the community, including the churches, schools and youth organizations which might influence those attitudes. The children attended one of three schools in and near 'Penvollard' which represent three types of education available for young children in Cornwall; a county school; a church school in a town and a rural church school. There were no church or grant maintained secondary schools in Cornwall so any lasting effect of primary education might be seen as the children progressed through the comprehensive school.

Cornwall is not in reality isolated from outside influences and the religiosity found there must be set in the context of religion in Britain as a whole. The religious map of Britain has changed in a variety of ways, not least with the growth of non-Christian religions and new religious movements. The religiosity of the non-worshipping majority also has to be considered in terms of non-organized beliefs and experiences and the civic religion of society as a whole. Chapter 1 asks how religious modern Britain is, by looking at different understandings of 'being religious' and regional variations. The decline in attendance at the main Christian churches means that those parents opting for a church school will be less likely than their own parents to be active church members but they will normally have received religious education at school. Assuming the school they attended kept to the provisions of the 1944 Education Act, religious instruction would have been part of the curriculum along with daily assemblies which were 'acts of worship'. The religious instruction was likely to have been Christian rather than multi-faith but it did not stem the decline in attendance at the main churches between the 1944 and 1988 Education Acts. Since 1944 each Local Education Authority has had to adopt an 'agreed syllabus' for religious education. The changing nature of these syllabuses in terms of

2

aims, content and methods is discussed in chapters 2 and provides a commentary on changing attitudes to religion, children and education.

Chapter 3 takes the story up from the 1988 Education Reform Act which brought conflicting ideas about the value and purpose of religious education and assemblies into the open. During the Parliamentary debate some members of both Houses of Parliament had the expectation that religious education and worship would 'make people good' but that concern is not necessarily shared by those more closely connected with the running of church schools. Varying views on the role of church schools, as expressed at national, diocesan and local level, are discussed in chapter 4. If a consensus could be found on what constitutes a 'good' church school then specific schools could be assessed against the suggested criteria. The problems of assessing whether a school achieves its goals centre on the methodology used to measure beliefs and attitudes. *Should* church schools have a positive effect on children's attitudes to religion and, if so, how could this be measured? If church schools have a distinctively Christian ethos or 'good' religious education how could these be recognised if not by some effect on the children who attend the school? Any measurement of religious attitudes and beliefs will be controversial because it involves judgements on matters which in Britain are seen as private and personal. If a school affects children's religiosity it could be construed as indoctrinating them.

The study of Penvollard in chapter 5 describes the community in which the families lived and the schools and churches the children attended, together with the aims of their teachers, governors and clergy. The views of the mothers and children themselves are sprinkled throughout the book but are looked at systematically in chapter 6. Although the study began with an interest in church schools it developed into a study of what the mothers termed 'normal' religion which is 'nice when they are young' but not seen as relevant in adulthood. The exceptions were the four mothers for whom religion was 'very important' whose stories are told in appendix 1. Since the children still attending regularly at age 16/17 came from these families the case studies may indicate the reasons why. Two of them, a born-again Christian and a Jehovah's Witness definitely fell outside the other mothers' definition of normal; for them their faith is their life and cannot be kept to a private sphere. Finally, chapter 7 considers the future for normal religion.

1 Religion in modern Britain

> I believe in God, you don't need to go to church, Christian I suppose I'd call myself ... I have a belief. I let the children evolve their own.

The mother quoted above had been sent to Sunday school as a child but had not attended since she was a teenager. However, she said she is religious, agrees that there is a benevolent power behind the universe and sees religious education as important and religious assemblies as 'no harm'. Like most children in Britain her son does not attend a church but he did receive religious education in school and attend a religious assembly on most school days. He had also belonged to the Boy's Brigade. From these sources he had gained some knowledge of religion, mainly Christianity. His favourite Bible story was one heard in a BBC broadcast at school.

What is typical about this mother and son is their acceptance of religious education in schools and tolerance to those who are religious as long as they are not prosletysing. Neither held specifically Christian beliefs but nor had they totally rejected the idea of God. The mother believed 'there has got to be someone up there' and the son said 'I do think whether there is one or not. If there was why would he let all the suffering go on?' Their lack of commitment to a particular religious group is also 'normal', committed members of any religious group are a small proportion of people in Britain. The mother's comment that her children should 'evolve their own' religious beliefs is not an unusually laissez faire statement, but, as will be seen in chapter 6, went along with a rejection of anything that might be seen as indoctrination in religion. Mothers who kept a close control over their young children's education and behaviour often left religious activity outside school 'up to them'. The British Social Attitudes survey asked parents how hard they would (or had) tried to get their children to share their own religious beliefs; the most frequent response was 'not at all hard' whereas when asked the same question about 'attitudes to right and wrong' the most frequent response was 'very hard' (British Social Attitudes, 1992, table N:2) Some politicians and religious groups see a necessary connection between religion and morality but the parents surveyed saw themselves having a role in passing on morality rather than religion.

Having started with an example of attitudes taken from interviews with one nominal Christian the aim of this chapter is to provide an overview of religion in Britain as a whole to provide the background to the religiosity of one group of families and their community which forms the core of the book. The focus is therefore on Christianity and on the religiosity of the nominally Christian. Much of the evidence which will be presented depends on what Barker termed 'head counting' (Barker, 1989, p. 34). That is, measuring religiosity in terms of external and observable aspects such as attendance at a place of worship and membership. Comparisons can be made across time and between different countries. Whatever the limitations of these statistics, including the need to be aware of the different definitions of membership and the purpose for which the figures were collected, they do provide a measure of the level of public participation in religion. Similarly, structured questionnaires and attitude scales have been used on large samples to provide information on religious beliefs. Again changes over time can be monitored and connections made with other variables such as social class, age and gender. Using the head counting approach there follows a description of religious practice and belief .

Religious practice

Mainstream Christian churches

Although most people say they have a religious affiliation this has to be put alongside a diminution of overall attendance at and membership of religious organizations (Krarup, 1983, p. 25, British Social Attitudes, 1991, p. 51). The statistics can show the extent to which people take part publicly in religious organizations and enable comparisons to be made over time but they cannot show what significance people attach to their membership or whether this too has changed. Using the available data the general picture is one of a decline in church attendance and the Christian rites of baptism, confirmation and marriage. Around two thirds of the British continue to identify with a denomination and express belief in God, although on these measures too there has been a decline from 1950s to today as detailed in Gallup polls, the Church of England Yearbooks and other large scale statistical surveys (Greeley, 1992)

The most extensive statistical survey of conventional religion in England and Wales was the 1851 census of religious worship which provides a point of comparison for modern figures of attendance despite the technical problems of collecting the data (Mann, 1853). As expected, churchgoing in 1851 was lower in towns and cities than in rural areas. The lowest figures for urban areas were in Sheffield and Manchester where total attendances were around a third of the total population and highest single attendances at a Church of England service were only five per cent and seven per cent respectively (Pickering, 1967, p. 403). In contrast Dorset had 30 per cent attendance at a Church of England and overall, in England and Wales, one out of every two adults (aged ten years and over) attended a place of worship (Pickering, 1967, pp. 394, 397). Contemporary commentators were not satisfied with those figures and Horace Mann, in his presentation of the census results, referred to 'the alarming number of the non-attenders' (Mann, 1853, p. clviii).

The most recent comparable study was the 1989 'English Church Census' which asked ministers and clergy to record attendance on Sunday October 15th 1989 and received an overall seventy per cent response rate (Brierley, 1991a). Estimating from these returns, 9.5 per cent of the adult population in England were in a place of Christian worship on that Sunday, compared with 11.3 per cent in a similar survey in 1979 (Brierley, 1991a, p. 30). The largest decline was in the Salvation Army (23 per cent less than in 1979) and, more significantly for overall attendance figures, a nine percent fall in Roman Catholic mass attendance since 1979 (Brierley, 1991a, pp. 32f, 43). These declines were to some extent offset by an increase in the Independent churches.

Surveys in Wales and Scotland have shown higher attendance, particularly in Scotland where attendance has been estimated at over fifteen per cent of adults (Brierley, 1991a, p. 203). Among children aged 14 and under, the English Church census recorded 13.7 per cent attendance, compared to 14 per cent in 1979 (Brierley, 1991a, p. 52). Generally fewer men attend a church than women, and the gap is increasing. The proportion of male attenders was 45 per cent in 1979 and three per cent less in 1989 (Brierley, 1991a, p. 85). In the Anglican Church the proportion had dropped six per cent to 39 per cent over the same period. Attendance is lowest among those in their twenties and thirties and although attendance has, in the past, increased as people grow older that cannot be assumed for each generation (Brierley, 1991a, 94f).

Occasional attendance at a religious service for a festival or 'rites de passage' is still common. A survey in Leeds found two thirds of the sample having attended in the last year, compared with a quarter who had attended a normal service (Krarup, 1983). Those most likely to attend were again women and those in higher social classes. More recently 51 per cent of the small Rural Church sample had attended a service at Christmas and 39 per cent at Easter, but with much lower male attendance (Davies et al, 1990, p. 68ff). At Easter women were twice as likely to attend as men. Christmas has replaced Easter as the highest point for attendance. Attendance is lowest among young adults, aged 18 to 35 years, at Christmas, Easter and Harvest as well as overall (Davies et al, 1990, p. 69). Irregular attendance has been found to be much more common in the Church of England than in other denominations, as it was in the 1851 Religious Census (Pickering, 1967, p. 395). Nearly 40 per cent of the English still consider themselves affiliated to the Church of England indicating the extent of nominal, or at best, fringe affiliates.

Rural areas may be seen as havens of religiosity but Francis's research in one rural diocese quoted a suggested figure of twelve per cent of people having contact with any church on a typical Sunday and only four per cent of the population who could be called active Christians (Francis, 1985, p. 42). The peak for involvement in an Anglican Church among children and young people was ages 6-9 and 10-13 (Francis, 1985, p. 56). John Hull described the age of eight as 'the high water mark of religiosity' (Hull, 1985, p. 8) and Francis found attitudes to Christianity became 'progressively less favourable' from age eight until the end of compulsory schooling in Local Authority schools, including voluntary aided schools (1984a, p. 8). The association of Christian practice with the very young will be explored in the Penvollard study.

In a separate study of a sample of Lancashire teenagers who did attend church, Francis found the ratio of girls attending to boys was roughly 6:4 throughout the teenage years (1984b, p. 29). Attendance declined 'quickly and consistently' from age 13 and 14 to age 20, so that on current trends over 70 per cent of 14 year old churchgoers would have ceased to attend by age 20. Teenagers going to an Anglican Church were less likely to go weekly than were those going to Free Church or Roman Catholic services, and the Church of England was least successful at keeping older teenagers (Francis, 1984b, p. 35). In terms of social class measured by fathers' and mothers' occupation, churchgoing teenagers were more likely to come from higher social classes compared with the general population, with 43 percent from social classes one or two (Francis, 1984b, p. 32).

The only Christian churches to gain members since 1979 were the African/West Indian churches (plus four per cent), the Pentecostal churches (plus eight per cent), the Independent churches (plus 42 per cent) and the Orthodox churches (plus 34 per cent), although the numbers are small in the last (9,400 adult churchgoers in 1989) (Brierley, 1991, pp. 35, 38). The House Church movement was the fastest growing with adult attendance more than doubling between 1979 and 1989, to reach over 100,000 (Brierley, 1991, p. 45). The numerous groupings are strong in particular areas, for example, Ichthus Fellowship in south east London, making the 'House Churches' the third major Christian presence in that area, after the Roman Catholics and Church of England. Their teaching was summed up in an article by the Archdeacon of Lewisham as; 'Evangelical, Charismatic and Baptist' (Church Times, 7.6.91). A proportion of those attending the newer independent churches have transferred from other denominations and it cannot be assumed that their growth will be sustained (Gill, 1993, p.219).

8

While individual religious practice is declining overall in Britain the majority are not anti-clerical or hostile to religion. Only ten per cent of those in a 1981 BBC survey who used to go to church but no longer do so, gave as their reason for no longer attending that they did not believe in Christianity anymore (White, 1988, p. 185). Most either said they 'had too much to do' or had 'lost the habit' and 'hardly anybody' blamed the clergy or Christians. In the 1982 Leeds survey only five per cent said they had stopped attending because they 'objected to the religious teaching' (Krarup, 1983, p. 30).

Non-Christian religions

The main non-Christian religions in Britain are Judaism, Islam, Hinduism, and Sikhism. Around 93 per cent of adherents live in England (Brierley and Longley, 1991, p. 240). All except Judaism have an increasing community size due mainly to immigration. The increase in active members of non-Christian religions between 1985 and 1990 is estimated to be fifteen per cent, in contrast to the four per cent decline in members of Christian churches over the same period. Islam is a permanent feature of British society with a Muslim community of 1.3 million meeting in over a thousand groups (Brierley and Longley, 1991, pp. 239f). The demand by some Muslim leaders that Muslim schools should be able to be granted voluntary aided status on the same basis as Anglican and Roman Catholic schools has been supported by the Roman Catholic Church and the Church of England Board of Education. Applications have so far been rejected mainly on the grounds that surplus places exist in neighbouring schools but questions have been raised about conformity to sex equality and the National Curriculum. The existence of private Muslim schools which teach the National Curriculum, the pressures from community leaders, including withdrawal of children from religious education, make it likely that an application will be granted in the near future (comment by Education Secretary in Times 17.1.96). Estimated community size for other non-Christian religions in Britain are 500,000 Sikhs, 400,000 Hindus and 300,000 Jews (Brierley and Longley, 1991, p. 240). Again continued growth in these religions cannot be assumed in the absence of large scale immigration into Britain. There is the possibility that nominal affiliations will increase and the rate of marriage outside the faith, as has been the case among the Jewish and Roman Catholic populations.

New Religious Movements

While sociologists and the religious organizations themselves try to explain why people do not attend the mainstream churches, they also try to explain why people do join one of the religious groups that have become known in

9

the west since the second world war. In the 'classic' model of industrialization secularization is one component of the industrial society, thus religiosity, other than residual attachment to a traditional form of religion, becomes a problem that has to be explained. New religious movements have tended to attract groups which have low participation in mainstream Christian churches: young adults and especially males. Numbers of members are generally small in Britain compared with the mainstream churches and groups are not available to join throughout the country. For example, two of the groups which have excited controversy are the Unification Church ('Moonies') with an estimated 350 members in 30 congregations and the Children of God with 500 members in 20 congregations (Brierley and Longley, 1991, pp. 238f). Longer established groups, the Mormons and Jehovah's Witnesses are both part of an international evangelising organization each with over 100,000 members Numbers in other groups are static or falling (Christedelphians, Church of Christ Scientist, New Church, Theosophists).

Regional Differences

Any national statistics on religion conceal regional differences. Church attendance levels in Northern Ireland and to a lesser extent, Scotland and Wales, are higher than they are in England. In Northern Ireland eight out of nine people said they belonged to a church according to a 1991 survey (Church Times, 21.10.94). The Church of Scotland, as the Established Church, helps to maintain the distinctive Scottish identity along with the legal and education systems (Dickson, 1989). The existence of a national church may help to explain both the higher level of regular attendance and membership, and the attendance of non-members who, in a Church of Scotland survey in 1987, reported attending church an average of nine times a year (Brierley, 1991a, pp. 21, 34). Religions other than Christianity are represented mainly in the large conurbations but Christian denominations are also unevenly spread throughout the country. In England the Anglican Church has the most churches, with over twice as many as any other denomination and over four times as many as the Catholic Church (Brierley, 1991a, p. 64). Through the parochial system and its schools, the Anglican Church still maintains a presence throughout England. The Roman Catholic Church is stronger in urban rather than rural areas and has, on average, larger congregations per church; in the 1989 'census' average attendance was 341 adults and children per Roman Catholic Church and only 70 for Anglican Churches (Brierley, 1991a, p. 47). Some Christian groups are strong only in specific areas, for example the Afro-Caribbean Churches in inner London, the Orthodox Church in Greater London and the House Church movement in south east England (Brierley, 1991a, p. 68ff). It may be that regional differences within

England will tend to be eroded with increased geographical mobility and there are already signs of such an erosion of Methodism in its south-west strongholds.

Religious Belief

Religious practice involves some degree of public display of an individual's religiosity. Another measurable aspect of religiosity is religious belief which is not necessarily linked to practice. If religious belief is measured by the individual's simple assent to questions, a wide circle of nominal believers may also be included. Belief in God remains high in Britain, around 70 per cent in recent surveys (Thompson, 1988, p. 228, Greeley, 1992, p. 55). However in the same surveys, belief in a personal God is lower, around 30 per cent and more believe in a 'spirit or life force'. In the 1981 European Values survey 'Indicators of Orthodox Belief', the average for Great Britain was slightly higher than the European average for belief in God, sin, soul, heaven, life after death, the devil and hell although only 27 per cent said they believed in all of these. Over three quarters of the sample had 'thought about whether there's a life after death' but less than half believed in it (Thompson, 1988). Nearly three quarters prayed at least occasionally, but most prayed alone and at home using their 'own thoughts' (Krarup, 1983, p. 49). Thus general religious beliefs are widespread but more specifically Christian beliefs and acceptance of the first three of the Ten Commandments are assented to by a minority (Krarup, 1983, p. 64f). The general religious beliefs could be the residue of more widespread Christian beliefs or could be evidence of a more general religiosity not related to traditional beliefs. Thompson (1988) quotes American studies as indicating that general beliefs and commitment vary 'directly with traditional beliefs' thus suggesting that as traditional Christian beliefs decline so too will the general beliefs. In the Penvollard study the percentage of adults who believed in God was the same as that found in large scale studies whereas the percentage for their children, age 12/13, was much lower (70%:49%).

Subjective approaches to measuring religiosity

'Head counting' approaches cannot set the individuals' response in a context which might help to explain them: for example, the beliefs and practices of family members and significant others, the influence of school, church and leisure activities in their community, all of which form a background to belief and practice recorded at one particular time in a response to a survey. Statistics can also not tell us, as Horace Mann wrote on the 1851 census, about 'the character and value of the adhesion represented by it' (Thompson, 1967, p. 96). The gap between 'believing' and 'belonging' is usually taken to indicate that the fall in church attendance may not mean that individuals are no longer religious: the high percentage believing in God or in favour of religion in schools being cited in support of this contention.   Thus David Martin pointed out that a decline in church attendance from the high point of Victorian times does not necessarily mean a decline in individual religiosity (Martin, 1967).   One reason could be the lack of social pressure to attend; as the 1981 BBC Research Report puts it: 'In a previous generation one went to church because 'everybody' went to church...' (Winter, 1988, p. 185).   However, one problem with this approach is that a majority may say they believe in a God but fewer subscribe to specifically Christian beliefs (or to those of any other religion). Belief in a personal God was only 37 per cent in the 1992 British Social Attitudes survey.   Neither do they engage in private religious activity (only 27 per cent pray weekly).   In any other area of investigation some more evidence would be required than assent to one question if an individual was to be claimed as belonging to a particular group.   For example to claim someone as environmentally concerned or 'green' something more than answering yes to the question, 'are you concerned about the environment' would be expected.   Perhaps the researcher would look for agreement with more specific statements and some evidence to back up the answers e.g. do you recycle waste, use public transport or a bicycle to go to work. Whatever significance can be attached to the numbers saying they believe in God it is clear that their God is the sort that can be ignored (Church Times, 20/10/95) .

If there is a need to look more deeply than the statistics for attendance and belief then as well as asking if those who *do not* attend may nevertheless be religious there is also the question of whether those who *do* attend do so for religious reasons.   Introducing their research in Leeds, Toon and Towler explain that it is;

> perfectly possible for there to be many non-religious members of a major religious group such as the Church of England (Toon, 1981, p. 8).

By this they mean that conventional organised religion may be participated in, not because of an acceptance of the teaching of that religion, but as a family activity or a way of gaining status.   If there are no 'supernatural referents' then such activity would be a form of 'surrogate' religion, an organised activity/interest/hobby (Toon, 1981, p. 7).   If in Britain even the regular churchgoers may not be 'really' religious there may not seem to be much religion to explain.   Looking first at the idea of church going to gain status, that was an accusation made by a few non-churchgoers in the

Penvollard study but only those who had experienced some pressure to attend. The following answer came from an 11 year old boy whose mother was a born again Christian and wanted him to attend;

> [Why do you think people go to church?] Because they are Christian or want to make themselves look honourable or high or good ... make other people look up to them. In the olden days you said 'I go to church' and [others] think 'he must be a good man'. Nowadays people still look up a bit .. I bet the Queen goes to church every Sunday and she's looked up to isn't she?

Another way in which church going could be a form of status seeking was found among those who attended church in order to get their child into the church school which was considered educationally and socially desirable. Parents are prepared to 'take to their knees to avoid the fees' (Church Times, 23.2.96).

The other suggested type of surrogate religion mentioned by Toon is the seeking of meaning through the family with the use of church affiliation. Dennison, Nash and Berger made a similar point when studying middle class American suburbanites who displayed what they called 'child-centred familism'. 'The Church is conceived as a necessary adjunct to the family (in this case, an ethical agency) in the task of socialising children' and parents join for the sake of their children, 'commitment to one's children is more important than a personal commitment to religion at the time of joining' (Dennison, Nash and Berger, 1972, p. 112f). The churches address themselves to the family, particularly to women and children. Tilby saw the child-centred church as mirroring the child-centred world and family festivals, such as Mothering Sunday and Christmas, becoming the popular services in the year (Tilby, 1979). Despite the low level of regular church going, families in Penvollard frequently referred to some form of religious practice as important for their young children. However this was often seen as provided by the school or Sunday school without the need for the family to attend altogether. Perhaps the British parent can rely on the school to provide this through religious assemblies whereas the exclusion of Christian practice from school in the USA focuses parent's attention on a church. One Penvollard family did attend church as 'an ethical agency', as the mother explained;

> I am not very religious minded, I don't want you to get the wrong idea. In [previous home] the Methodist was opposite where we lived. It was a very active church and the children went and were in the Sunday school. The same thing happened when we moved here.

The family moved again but by then the older children were away from home and the family did not go to another church. The church had been useful both for social activities and for reinforcing the morality which the mother considered important. It had something to offer at a particular stage of family life. The mother said, 'Christian beliefs and the way of bringing up children are important ... that side of the church that is important, morality'.

Once subjective understanding becomes the key to understanding religious behaviour, and religion is seen as something which gives meaning to peoples' lives, it is a short step to defining as religious anything which gives meaning to an individual's existence. Thus Berger and Luckmann employed an inclusive definition of religion in which religion played a 'decisive part in the construction and maintenance of universes' or systems of meaning (Berger and Luckmann, 1969, p. 63). Traditional institutional religion is one form of legitimation but individuals can choose different 'ultimate meanings', as they can choose goods, friends and marriage partners. Luckmann suggested the central theme of ultimate significance to be that of the 'autonomous individual' (Luckmann, 1967). According to Luckmann, the likelihood of individuals being socialised into traditional forms of religion declines the more 'modern' are the factors in their socialization (Luckmann, 1967, p. 100). John Hull developed that point and argued that religion is used by many as a haven from modernity. Those most likely to take part in it are those peripheral to modern society; particularly young children and the elderly (Hull, 1985). Other groups may acknowledge the incompatibility between modernity and their religion and shut themselves off from the wider society rather than learn from it, although they may appear modern by, for example, using modern technology in worship.

The value accorded to the autonomous individual was a theme found in Penvollard although mothers asserted the value more in relation to their children than to themselves (see chapter 6). It may explain the criticism of people undertaking missionary work in the community which was found among the families in the study. As well as making a public display of their views local missionaries are invading the private haven of the home and trying to influence the views of other people. There is tolerance for individual, private belief but criticism of churchgoers. The important aspects of Christianity are to do with helping other people and are not achieved by churchgoing. The description of regular churchgoers as 'hypocrites' seems to stem from their public performance of what is perceived to be an unnecessary part of religion. A mother criticises missionary work and emphasises what is important;

14

coming to the house and being asked to go to church ... My husband is better for doing things on the quiet than the Jehovah's Witnesses knocking on doors. He runs a boy's football team and helps neighbours.

This practical view of Christianity is one found in other studies . (Bruce, 1995, p. 53).

Religious experience

If individual consciousness is the focus one aspect of religion which assumes importance is individual spiritual experience. These can be simply counted as they were by a question in a 1985 Gallup Poll which found 41 per cent of women and 31 per cent of men claimed that they had had a religious experience (Hay, 1987, p. 124). Many of those people had told no one about the experience because of a fear of ridicule (Hay, 1987, p. 163). In the British Social Attitudes survey 28 per cent said they had 'felt close to a powerful spiritual force that seemed to lift you out of yourself' (Greeley, 1992, p. 56). A questionnaire study by Robinson and Jackson aimed to 'learn more about the religious or spiritual ideas, feelings and experiences of young people' aged 16 to 19 years (Robinson and Jackson, 1987, p. 3). They focused on 'living, individual experience' and include both conventional religious beliefs and practices and;

> those ideas and feelings which might be regarded as contributing to a wider and less explicit, perhaps even unconscious, religiosity. (Robinson and Jackson, 1987, p. 6)

The authors acknowledged that it is 'impossible ... to do justice to the individuality of human experience by any kind of quantitative research' but that such a method did allow comparisons to be made between young people from different educational and social backgrounds (Robinson and Jackson, 1987, p. 3). The questionnaire included two model passages, based on accounts sent in to the Alister Hardy Research Centre, the first referred to feelings arising from seeing beauty in nature ending with the words, 'you feel you are somehow part of a mysterious whole' (Robinson and Jackson, 1987, p. 12). The second passage referred specifically to God and began; 'At times of great difficulty or danger in my life I have felt I can always pray to God and get help' (Robinson and Jackson, 1987, p. 12). Out of the six and a half thousand young people in the sample 79 per cent said that they had had an experience 'very' or 'fairly' like that in the first passage. However responses to the explicitly theistic extract were divided 53:47 per cent between 'very' or 'fairly' like and 'not at all' (Robinson and Jackson, 1987, p. 12). As in earlier research, positive response was higher among females and was related to educational achievement, especially for the mystical experience.

The problem of assessing the significance of evidence of 'spiritual experiences' in any study of religion in Britain, remains. One conclusion drawn in Robinson and Jackson's study is that young people who have a low response to established forms of religion may have a positive response to implicit religion (Robinson and Jackson 1987, p. 71). About two-fifths score high on the implicit religion scale but low on the explicit religion scale. Whether this is seen as significant depends on the definition of religion that is preferred, but a high rating on the implicit religion scale does not imply any commitment to organised religion or to any theistic belief. Both the implicit religion scale and the mystical experience scale do imply a willingness to reflect on experience and a 'sense of mystery' which, from the point of view of organised religion, could be seen as a foundation on which to build. However, new religious movements depend on some initial interest in spiritual questions but only attract a small proportion of young people in Britain. Churches, which are familiar to most young people if only from the outside, may be seen as places appealing for funds, running social events, weddings and carol services rather than places one would go to for spiritual guidance. Barker reported that young people said they found it difficult to get teachers or clergy to 'discuss, let alone answer, their most important and ultimate questions' (Barker, 1983, p. 46). Mothers in the Penvollard study raised questions from 'why does God let people suffer?' (adults and children) to 'who did Adam and Eve's children marry?' (an adult). They were claiming that the churches 'never tell you that', rather than being dissatisfied with answers they had heard.

New Age beliefs and practices might be more attractive for those with an unfocused sense of mystery. Individuals can buy a book, visit a therapist, attend a workshop, finding something that suits them without necessarily having to make any regular commitment.

Civil religion

Religion may be significantly involved in society's institutions; in education, politics and social affairs both directly and through religious values. The churches are involved in primary, secondary and higher education and all schools must make provision for religious education and worship. Over a quarter of maintained primary school places are in voluntary aided or controlled schools, mainly Roman Catholic or Church of England. Many leisure activities for young children still have a religious element; the uniformed organizations of Brownies, Guides, Cubs and Scouts, Girls' and Boys' Brigades and Cadet groups for the different armed forces. Christian ritual is part of ceremonies of Parliament and national events. John Habgood, Archbishop of York, sees religious institutions as

16

continuing to be important in Britain (Habgood, 1983). He argues that religion is still significant as an important source of values 'on which the conduct of public life depends' and provides a public language of 'hope, aspiration, penitence and renewal'. There is still 'a formal public commitment to the Christian faith, expressed in part through the Monarchy', although the attitudes to the monarchy are changing with the events of the 1990s (Habgood, 1983, p. 49). Bryan Wilson also focused on religious institutions but argued that society is secularised. The continuing use of religious symbols and language in public life was interpreted by Wilson as 'the borrowed capital of its religious past' (Wilson, 1982).

Although a state can be secular it cannot be value-free. For Durkheim the basic shared values of society, its morality, are upheld and reaffirmed through rituals which bind people together (Durkheim, 1915, p. 47). In Britain rituals associated with the Royal family and other national events have been seen as expressing shared values (Shils and Young, 1953, Bailey, 1985, p. 24). In this perspective civil religion uses Christian symbolism to celebrate and reinforce shared values. Popular civil religion includes 'all those happenings that bring people together, and all those activities to which individuals are devoted' which form part of the shared national identity even though all individuals may not support them with enthusiasm (Bailey, 1985, p. 25). Those in public life may find support in religious teaching for their own views and religious leaders may themselves be divided over what are appropriate and inappropriate applications of their faith. Thus there were criticisms from church leaders over services to celebrate victory in war and Christian teaching has been used by politicians to back up varied views on the problems of the inner city and the importance of individual responsibility and morality. Divisions within the churches and between the Church of England and the Government receive extensive coverage in the media, as in debates over crime, housing, poverty and education.

It is assumed by writers on civil religion that society is held together by shared beliefs and ritual practices, which in a complex differentiated society will be general rather than specific. Changes in the way religious values are expressed are inevitable as 'new gods' must take the place of the 'old gods' as society changes. Individuals may be committed to one of many diverse forms of religion or to none and yet still share basic values. It has been argued that many sects in America share the same moral values; they uphold the American way of life, stressing individual achievement, success and motivation (Herberg, 1955). Luckmann considers doctrinal differences as virtually irrelevant among Protestant denominations (Luckmann, 1967). A Church of England survey of young peoples' attitudes, 'A Kind of Believing' found that they stressed the individual's right to believe anything they like. People must have freedom to explore for themselves and arrive at their own conclusions (Hare Duke and

Whitton, 1977, p. 22). In discussions on spirituality involving Devon secondary school teachers, mainly of religious education, one session focused on the question of whether there are shared basic values in society (Neal, 1982, pp. 22f). All the teachers assumed that British society was pluralist and that when society celebrates together, at Christmas or Royal Weddings, the apparent cohesion is a myth; people are not celebrating 'real' values. The teachers were concerned that they should offer alternatives to children and not indoctrinate them or abuse their position of influence. Like the young people reported in 'A Kind of Believing' these teachers said that individuals should make up their own minds about the values they would live by (Neal, 1982, p. 23). The theme of the autonomous individual who can make choices is, of course, a theme in all areas of modern society including education and health. It was a theme to which most of the Penvollard mothers subscribed and will be discussed further in chapter 6. For religious individualists religion will be freely chosen by each person rather than passed from generation to generation (Roof and Gesch, 1995, p. 74).

Conclusions

Conventional organised religion in Britain regularly involves a small percentage of the population but the majority will be involved occasionally at festivals or rites de passage. Most children participate in religious education and worship in schools and Christianity is still central to national events. There is evidence for what has been termed 'common religion', defined as unorganised beliefs and practices associated with the supernatural, the unexplained and the mysterious and for religious experiences (Toon, 1981, p. 6). Thus church based religion, civil/public religion and individualised religious beliefs and experiences all exist in modern Britain but are inextricably intertwined.

Individuals can choose from a variety of sets of ideas which may or may not lead them to join a religious organization. The Leeds studies found some respondents had an eclectic set of beliefs, which did not necessarily correspond with any particular religious group (Krarup, 1983). The simplest explanation for individuals joining any religious group is that they feel it will answer a need. It is more difficult to find separate kinds of spiritual needs which can only be met by a religious group. The kinds of spiritual experiences reported in the Robinson and Jackson included those evoked by the beauty of nature. The countryside and nature may have 'become one of the principal vehicles of the sacred' and 'imbued with a quasi-religious significance' but, as Anthony Russell concludes, this is a 'religion without God' (Russell, 1986, p.45). People might join an

18

environmental group rather than a religious one to meet some spiritual needs.

Fewer people are brought up and remain in the same religious group all their lives and a smaller percentage of people become members of a religious organization as children. The churches will continue to become more similar to sects and new religious movements, with members who have chosen to join as adults and a shrinking group of 'fringe' members. Although some groups pay close attention to the socialization of members' children, such as the Jehovah's Witnesses, the mainstream churches are concerned that 'nurture' should not be seen as indoctrination, as shown in discussions on Anglican schools (see chapter 4). The decrease in attendance at a 'Sunday school' may be partly due to parents sharing the concern that children should not be 'sent' or 'made to go', although parents at the same time generally support religion in school. This ambivalence leads back to the point that most adults in Britain have not rejected the content of religion and it is still seen as good for children. John Hull suggests;

> As adults and parents we socialise our children into that for which we have a fond nostalgia but can no longer take seriously ourselves. (Hull, 1985, p. 8)

That could be one reason for parental support for religious education and worship in schools, particularly for the special occasions they will remember like nativity plays and harvest festival, and the persistence of a higher rate of church attendance among young children compared with adults. Along with puerilization of religion comes feminization, with a preponderance of women in the pews and girls in Sunday schools/youth churches and as confirmation candidates. Penvollard Methodist Church archives provide evidence of an excess of males in youth activities in the recent past. Evidence suggests that rather than the male sex being inherently less religious it seems to be their ('traditional') role in the family that encourages a view of Christianity as the province of women and young children now that it is no longer normal or socially desirable to practise (Levitt, 1995b, p. 535).

Religious education and assemblies will be for most children the most regular, or only, contact with mainstream religions. Although there is provision for parents to opt out, only Jehovah's Witness parents have done so as a body. However, a withdrawal of Muslim pupils, from RE but not collective worship, in one area of West Yorkshire may herald a change in attitude among Muslim leaders (Times, 22.1.96). Given that most children, of all faiths or none, do take part in religious education as their parents did, it is important to examine its changing nature. In 1944 Biblically based instruction in schools was intended to lead children to a personal Christian

19

faith. Under the 1988 legislation 'religious instruction' becomes 'religious education' and every agreed syllabus must 'take account of the teaching and practices of the other principal religions represented in Great Britain' (Education Reform Act, 1988, chapter 40). In the 1980s syllabuses Christian nurture was to be undertaken by the churches while religious education was to be justified on educational grounds. However religion owes its privileged position in schools to the perception of its role in providing a moral framework through assemblies and classroom work rather than to a recognition that children should understand and be tolerant of a variety of religions. The next chapter explores the development of modern religious education since 1944.

2 Religion in education: 1944-1988

Religious education is an important part of children's education ...

I agree. You learn about beliefs and then she can make up her own mind ...
I agree, as a basis for forming an opinion ...
I think so even though I am not a religious person. They have got to do everything and then make up their own minds later as they grow up. I am not one to lead against any belief, not having a strong, keen belief myself ...

These three comments from nominally Christian mothers on the statement, 'Religious education is an important part of children's education' suggest a desire for a phenomenological, objective approach to the subject. They wanted their children to know about different beliefs but had no strong feelings about the end result of the teaching. They assumed that children should be taught about 'beliefs' not just Christianity. The importance of each individual freely choosing was evident among most mothers who were practising Christians as well; 'You can't believe strongly unless you know about other beliefs, you need to know and question'. However, others felt that non-Christian faiths should come later on, especially in an area where they were not represented. None of them had studied non-Christian religions in their own religious education which would still have been 'Christian education' in the 1960s. All saw a different role for religious education in school and Christian education in the churches. Such a distinction was not made until the syllabuses of the 1960s (later in Cornwall). For the earlier compilers of syllabuses the aim of RE in school was to nurture young Christians.

For a generation from 1944, religious instruction was the only compulsory school subject. The 1944 Education Act left it to Local Education Authorities to decide how to fulfil their duty to provide 'efficient education to meet the needs of the population of their own' (Education Act, 1944, section 11.7). In 1947 'The New Secondary Education' specifically stated that 'neither the subjects of the curriculum nor the time spent on each, nor the way they are to be taught is laid down by the Ministry of Education'. The exception of religious education pointed both to the value attached to it and to its controversial nature. The agreed syllabuses reflect current educational thinking and local concerns and the changes in syllabuses which applied to Penvollard will be compared with general developments in syllabuses in England as a whole. From a similar pre-war starting point Cornwall produced syllabuses that maintained some independence from the general changes in religious education, until the 1989 syllabus and handbook which brought it back into line with other parts of the country.

Syllabuses pre-1944

Before the 1944 Education Act, religious instruction was not required to be taught, but any such teaching was subject to the Cowper-Temple clause of 1870 which stated that it should be non-denominational. Syllabuses were drawn up by agreement between churches and local authorities. In 1936 the Cornwall County Education Committee issued the 1930 York syllabus under their own cover. Typical of syllabuses of this period its content was entirely Bible based and studied the foundation of the Christian faith. For infants there were 'simple stories from the Life of our Lord' and a few Old Testament stories chosen to be 'uplifting'. The junior and senior sections comprised a systematic study of the Bible with the emphasis on the New Testament. Centred on a study of the past the teaching was directed at the nurture of young Christians.

> Practical Christianity, in fact, will be the great and supreme test of the effectiveness of the teaching (Cornwall Education Committee, 1936, p. 8).

It was emphasised throughout that the details were relatively unimportant and teachers must be careful not to overload children with detail. Religious instruction was said to provide the 'great opportunity for the teacher to lift his pupils above the detail and drudgery which must form a part of the process of education, as of life itself', a comment which may have been a reference to earlier syllabuses, some of which simply consisted of materials to be memorised (Cornwall Education Committee, 1936, foreword). Nevertheless it is clear that there was a danger that once children knew some Bible passages and the Ten Commandments religious instruction was seen as having been satisfactorily undertaken. The teacher was now advised to keep abreast of modern thought as well as expressing his religious faith through the subject matter he teaches and 'naturally ... to 'pray about his work'. Beliefs about what was supposed to come out of religious teaching in schools have changed greatly since that time.

Agreed syllabuses 1944 -1960s

After 1944 the practice in some respects was very similar. Each Local Education Authority had to adopt an existing syllabus or draw up their own through an Agreed Syllabus Conference consisting of four groups; the Church of England, other denominations depending on the area, representatives of teachers' associations and the local authority itself (Cox and Cairns, 1989). These four committees had to agree unanimously on the syllabus to be used in local authority and controlled schools. In practice little change was immediately discernible in agreed syllabuses. The Cambridgeshire syllabus, written soon after the end of the Second World War, described the social and individual problems facing the country and proposed Christianity as the remedy (1951, pp. 1-9). No man-made ideal, including democracy, could inspire 'free citizens' to serve it unless it was founded on 'something greater' (Cambridgeshire syllabus, 1951, p. 7). Christianity should not be used as a way to back up democratic principles but because democratic principles are fruitless if they are not grounded in Christian faith. The introduction ended with a summary of the active purpose of teaching the Christian religion;

> To teach Christianity to our children is to inspire them with the vision of the glory of God in the face of Jesus Christ, and to send them into the world willing to follow Him who was among us as one who serveth, because they know that in such service alone is perfect freedom. (Cambridgeshire syllabus, 1951,p. 9)

In the intervening years this aim has been substantially changed but was re-echoed by Baroness Cox and her supporters in the parliamentary debate on religious education in the 1988 Education Reform Act (see pages 36ff). Ironically her opponents supported a retention of the provisions of the 1944 Education Act because the content of religious instruction was not specified and nothing was said about the form regular worship should take, thus leaving the way open for multi-faith religious education and assemblies. Looking at the syllabuses which came out immediately after 1944 it is obvious that Christianity and Christian worship were to be taught and the syllabus conferences did not provide for the representation of those of non-Christian faiths. Christianity may not have been specified because of the assumption that Britain was, or should be, a Christian country and that Christianity had brought people together in the crises of the Second World

War. Although church attendance was in decline, it has been argued that this was because churchgoing was replaced with other activities rather than because Christianity was being rejected (Cox and Cairns, 1989, p. 3). The same argument has been used in relation to churchgoing at the end of the twentieth century but this could be seen as a symptom rather than a cause of decline (Gill, 1993, p.188). Other activities are more attractive on a Sunday to those not committed to attending a church.

Agreed syllabuses used in Cornwall 1946 and 1964

In 1946 a supplement to the syllabus echoed the sentiments of the Cambridgeshire syllabus with a clear link made between the teaching of the Bible and service to others. In addition to the Biblical material of 1936 there was material on Church history and the Church in Cornwall. Because of the narrow focus of the syllabus it covered material more thoroughly than later versions. Its central purpose was the nurture of young Christians through a knowledge of the Bible, the history of the Church and, most importantly, the teachers' own spirituality. In modern eyes the syllabus might appear to be concentrating entirely on the teaching of knowledge but the value of teaching was not to be measured by the ability of children to recall facts and memorise passages rather it could 'only be gauged by the love of God which is inculcated, together with its corollary, love to our neighbours'.

The 1964 Agreed Syllabus in Cornwall was also based on Bible centred themes rather than Goldman experiential ones popular in the later 1960s and early 1970s. The infant and junior sections consisted entirely of lists of Biblical references under headings. In the infant section two headings were; 'Old Testament Stories' and 'Loving Deeds of Jesus', and in the junior section; 'The childhood of Jesus' and 'Preparation for the ministry' (Cornwall Education Committee, 1964, pp. 95f, 100). Both sections contained suggested passages for memory work. For juniors there was one section on 'later followers of Jesus' and one on 'Modern Christians', although the definition of modern ranged from John Bunyon in the seventeenth century to Dr. Barnardo in the nineteenth century (Cornwall Education Committee, 1964, pp. 101,105.).

The arrangement of work year by year was retained in the secondary section. In the first three years the Bible was to be studied more systematically. The fourth year was 'felt to be the heart of the syllabus', since the majority of children would leave at the end of that year (Cornwall Education Committee, 1964, p. 107). There the stress changed to Christian belief and conduct although aimed at convincing pupils of the truth of Christian belief rather than looking at how Christians worship. Perhaps the assumption was that teenagers might question the beliefs but they still knew about the practices, or, that any detail of practice might divide the main denominations in the county; Methodist and Church of England. The course on 'The Christian Faith' for fourth years had a traditional version based on the Apostles' Creed and an alternative more child-centred course based on questions submitted by local children. Those questions received answers containing Biblical, theological and philosophical arguments all directed at convincing pupils of the truth of Christian beliefs. The question 'Is God a real person, a fantasy or a process?' was answered by the argument that someone must be behind the process that started the creation of the universe; 'if anyone argues that God is fantasy, they must do a lot of explaining to account for the universe' (Cornwall Education Committee, 1964, p. 107). The fifth year course looked at the history of the church, early Christian society and the Churches today. The sixth form course contained more advanced Bible study, including St. John's gospel, and some theology. Only one side of notes on 'Christianity in Action' considered contemporary Christianity. World religions were mentioned as a possible alternative for sixth form work .

Interestingly no specific aims were given for different age groups, which again placed this syllabus among the older type rather than among those which in the next few years would be influenced by developmental psychology. General aims included;

> We must ensure that Religious Education does not become simply an account of man's quest for religious experience and truth [rather it is] Religious Education which will expound and illuminate the Christian faith that we are concerned with. (Cornwall Education Committee, 1964, p. 5)

Daily worship, providing the opportunity for Christian witness, was therefore 'the most important aspect of religious education'. It was acknowledged that school assembly would be the only experience of worship for some children but confidently stated that;

> Young people full of the joy of living respond readily to the invitation to join in praise and thanksgiving. (Cornwall Education Committee, 1964, p. 16)

Religious education is seen as working alongside the churches, it 'will supplement their work by extending to the materials they use the humble enquiry and honest study which the best teachers see as their tools' (Cornwall Education Committee, 1964, pp. 11f).

Later a clear distinction would be drawn in both agreed syllabuses and reports from the churches between the work of school and church, but at this time the teacher was assumed to be a practising Christian whose faith was important. There was still the emphasis on the teachers' commitment and spirituality:

> The teacher will equip himself as best he can, do his best and say his prayers and like the Lord, whose faith he tries to teach struggle for success ... and hope that the germinating seed of God's Word will fall on the good ground of God's growing children. (Cornwall Education Committee, 1964, p. 12)

'Child-centred' religious education

The syllabuses of the later 1960s were influenced by developments in educational thinking, both in terms of attitudes to those who taught and to those who were taught. The Plowden report which examined primary education endorsed 'child-centred' primary education in which the child would be 'the agent in his own learning' (Central Advisory Council for Education, 1967). It was not enough to specify what children ought to know without considering the children themselves and their lives and experiences. Religion, like any other topic, must be taught in a way that was relevant to modern living. Goldman's research, published in 1964, identified stages in childrens' religious development using the insights of Piaget (Goldman, 1964). Goldman recommended limited formal teaching for infant pupils. Teachers should start instead with the children's own questions about the world (Goldman, 1965, p. 88). For the junior school he advocated the teaching of religious education through life-themes based on an area of the child's experience; homes, friends or hands for first year juniors; holidays, the seasons or gifts for second year juniors and Myself, Creation or Growth for 9-11 year olds (Goldman, 1965, p. 11, 141). He stressed the use of discussion methods for adolescents based on specific problems, whether using Bible or Life-themes, and intended 'to get the pupils to think genuinely for themselves in their encounter with Christian belief' (Goldman, 1965, p. 187).

Parallel developments in popular theology centred on John Robinson's 'Honest to God', published in 1963, which was based on his selection from the ideas of Bultmann, Bonhoeffer and Tillich (Robinson, 1963 pp. 21ff). He proclaimed that Christianity must show it is 'relevant' to modern man and the image of God as 'out there' must go;

> For I want God to be as real for our modern secular, scientific world as he ever was for the 'ages of faith'. (Robinson and Edwards, 1963, p. 279)

26

The change of name of the Christian Education Movement's journal from 'Religion in Education' to 'Learning for Living', in 1961 under the editorship of Harold Loukes, illustrated the change in religious education at that time. Key words were now 'child-centred' and 'relevant'. Religious education was to help the child on a personal 'quest for meaning' with the teacher as a guide rather than an instructor. The new style syllabuses used child-centred themes and abandoned a year by year arrangement of content in favour of broader categories. The West Riding Syllabus began by stating the needs of the child; for security, significance, standards and community; rather than theological or social justifications for religious education (West Riding of Yorkshire Education Department, 1966, p. 3). Wiltshire published two syllabuses in the same handbook. One, the new approach and one an old style Bible based syllabus (Wiltshire Education Committee, 1967).

The implicit approach, deriving from Loukes, centred on the child's personal quest for meaning. The child would be personally involved; learning was self-initiated; it affected the learners' behaviour and attitudes; it was evaluated by the learner rather than externally and it was meaningful to the individual learner. Loukes made the distinction between what was taught and how it was taught. Thus something apparently religious, like the Nativity or Passion stories could be;

> as irreligious as quadratic equations if they are treated on the surface. (Schools Council 1971, p. 36)

On the other hand a 'lesson on spiders; an argument on Charles 1, a study of the climate of Peru' were;

> all as 'religious' as the story of Abraham if they are treated personally and set the hearers off into the depth. (Schools Council, 1971, p. 36)

Looking at the school syllabus of religious education or programme of projects for the term would not, in that view, identify whether children were being educated religiously.

Although the child-centred approach was the orthodoxy after Plowden among policy makers and educationalists it is doubtful whether it was ever the norm among the majority of classroom teachers (Simon and Garron, 1975, Bennett, 1976). The influence of Plowden and Goldman could be seen in the new agreed syllabuses, although implicit child-centred religious education was advocated alongside 'explicit' material and emphasised more for the younger children and perhaps the sixth form. It is difficult to ascertain how classroom teaching changed, particularly in secondary schools with the influence of examination syllabuses. A 1971 report in the

A.M.A. journal gave an estimate from School Correspondents of 17 per cent of schools in which religious education was 'closely related' to the agreed syllabus (British Journal of Religious Education, Spring 1979, p. 96). In a 1979 survey of North Yorkshire secondary schools less than a quarter of Heads of Department used any books about the teaching of religious education when planning their courses. Only 16 per cent mentioned using the 1966 West Riding Syllabus which was still the relevant one for those schools and which had a child-centred developmental approach with the emphasis on religion in the contemporary world and the need for pupils to discover Christianity for themselves (British Journal of Religious Education, Spring 1979).

The model of teacher as Christian 'nurturer' rather than 'professional' was, in other areas, being affected by the stress on religious education as requiring subject specialists and a professional approach. A National Teachers' Committee for Religious Education was formed by the Christian Education Movement in the 1960's, and became a member of the Council of Subject Teaching Associations (British Journal of Religious Education, Spring 1984, p.59). The distinction between 'nurturer' or 'indoctrinator' and 'professional' is questionable. It seems to assume that people with specialist qualifications are only putting information in children's way so they can make their own judgements, a model far removed from the everyday life of a school. The teacher will not always control the topics and questions which arise in the classroom and may not feel able to accept all opinions which children express. If the teacher first establishes 'ground rules', for example on respecting other peoples' faiths or not using racist language then already some opinions will be stifled. The material introduced by the teacher will be only one influence on the children's judgements and they will not necessarily be formed by critical, rational and open thought processes.

Agreed Syllabus for Cornwall 1971

This syllabus, which reflected the child-centred approach in its junior and infant section, was published in 1971 and written 'by teachers for the use of teachers' (Cornwall Education Committee, 1971). It was apparent that the Bible had become subordinate to the child's own experience, to be used 'where it is relevant to the experience being explored'. Education could be religious without the Bible being 'forced into the theme at every point'. For the first time, the way children learn was discussed. It was stated that too much material was often taught to children too early and that junior school children think in a concrete way finding the formation of abstract concepts 'very difficult if not impossible' (Cornwall Education Committee, 1971, junior section, p. 1). The aim of religious education was taken from the 1970 Durham report, The Fourth R, and was said to be not 'conversion but enlightenment', a distinction not made in earlier syllabuses. It is stressed that the child will make the decision to accept or reject Christianity, that the decision should be based on an 'accurate, unprejudiced understanding' and that those who do reject it must be given something on which to base a personal philosophy. In the earlier syllabus the school was to endeavour to 'illuminate and expound the Christian religion', not to contribute to the formation of alternative personal philosophies, even as a second best Cornwall Education Committee, 1964, p. 5). In 1971, topics for infants included Families, Friends, Helpfulness and Compassion. Poems and stories were referenced, although a link to the Bible was always made.

The aim of the Durham report seemed to allow for the non-believing 'professional' teacher but the syllabus still assumed that the non-specialist primary teacher would be a Christian as the syllabus and 'notes for teachers' before each theme were addressed to believers. Children were also assumed to be Christian. Thus in the theme of 'Friends' it was stated that the theme 'can be used as a starting point for the consideration of prayer i.e. we talk to our friends, and we talk to God as a friend' (Cornwall Education Committee, 1971, Infant section, p. 8). It continues; 'Discuss how we pray. Why do we pray? Does God always answer? Is 'no' or 'wait' an answer? How Jesus told us to pray' (Cornwall Education Committee, 1971, Infant section, p. 9).

The section on assembly emphasised the importance of integrating worship with classroom work. The starting point was now to be the child's work. In earlier syllabuses school worship was, like church worship, based on a set pattern with the Bible and the Lord's prayer central to it. By 1971, the Bible was to be used 'where relevant to the theme' and prayers written by the children are 'a vital part of the worship of the school'. It was suggested that a display of children's work on the theme they were working on can provide 'a vital link between work and worship'. Classroom worship was recommended so children 'will feel free to take an active part'.

The secondary section, while showing the influence of modern ideas, had changed more radically in its presentation than in its content. This may have reflected the fact that it was written by practising religious education teachers who might tend to use their own tested approaches rather than to reflect the latest ideas. The section contained no overall aim for religious education but said it should be an equal partner with the other subjects on the curriculum 'because the philosophy of the school is Christian', rather than be included only as a statutory requirement in which case it 'is highly probable that it will be a waste of everybody's time' (Cornwall Education Committee, 1971, secondary section, p. 1). It is interesting to note the belief of teachers that a state secondary school would have a Christian philosophy. School worship was said to be a 'challenging, thought provoking spiritual exercise' and 'educationally sound' (secondary section, p. 3). It was perhaps assumed in the earlier 1964 syllabus that Christian worship was educationally sound. The definition of worship was a little broader than in the last syllabus, finding room for pupils' own 'deep concern' about the ills of society and using sources and traditions 'not necessarily exclusively Christian'. The latter comment was omitted from the 1976 edition.

Generally the secondary syllabus for Cornwall was, in 1971, less academic and intellectual than in 1964. It was presented thematically including Bible themes using material similar to the previous syllabus and a topic on 'Modern Problems' covering some of the same subjects as 'Christian conduct' did in 1964. The topic on Modern Problems was presented as a series of questions, for example, 'Is there a basic unchangeable code [of morality]?' There were no Biblical references given (Cornwall Education Committee, 1971, secondary section, p. 37). There was less systematic Bible teaching and more emphasis on the relevance of Christianity to modern living. There was some material on religions other than Christianity in one topic in the secondary section. The Christian religion was taken first and then other views set out.

Although the more modern syllabuses, such as West Riding (1966) and ILEA (1968) looked very different from earlier Bible centred syllabuses the aims were still to help children to a Christian commitment but focused on their own concerns and questions. The next major change was to come with the 'phenomenological' approach and the inclusion of world religions throughout the syllabuses. The Shap working party, founded in 1969, was influential in curriculum development through its annual mailing, including the calendar of world religions, and in-service courses, and the work of Ninian Smart who became its president (Smart 1971, 1973).

The 'phenomenological' approach

By the mid-sixties immigration into Britain, mainly from Commonwealth countries, had led to an increased presence of children from different cultural and religious backgrounds in some areas. The distinction between seeking to convert children to Christianity and giving them knowledge and understanding was already being made by professional and church organizations and in agreed syllabuses. The Durham Commission (1970), the British Council of Churches and the Christian Education Movement all stressed that children must make up their own minds on the basis of their religious education;

> To press for acceptance of a particular faith or belief system is the duty and privilege of the Churches and other similar religious bodies. It is certainly not the task of a teacher in a county school. (Durham Commission, 1970, p. 103)

30

One widely quoted aim for religious education incorporating that view came from Jean Holm in 1975;

> To help pupils to understand what religion is and what it would mean to take a religion seriously. (Holm, 1975, p. 7)

Earlier syllabus writers would have considered the aim of leading children to Christianity as educationally justifiable for all children but the stress on learning by discovery and experiment in other subjects implied a change in religious education. Another factor was the presence of children from non-Christian backgrounds in some schools. It is only in the last two decades that people havé been so aware of the increased numbers of non-Christian children attending schools and the existence of Church schools with non-Christian majorities is more recent still. Teaching them 'about' Christianity could be justified on cultural and historical grounds but raised the question of whether the other children should be taught about the faiths now practised in their locality. The alternative would have been to separate children so that they could be taught about the faith of their own homes or not to teach religion at all. It would be difficult to arrange 'own faith' teaching within the school day (although some schools hold withdrawal classes particularly for Muslim children) and it would also have been a return to the school doing the work of the churches rather than educating children about religion. To abolish religious education in school would have entailed a change in the law which given the successful lobby for a strengthening of the position of religious education and worship in the 1988 Act would not have succeeded. Earlier attempts by humanists had also been unsuccessful.

The approach to religious education termed 'phenomenological' or 'explicit' was seen as suitable for a situation where, even if the children in a particular school were not from different faiths, people were more aware of alternatives to Christianity and less certain that they were all in error. Children were to be encouraged to 'put themselves in other people's shoes' and learn about others' faiths without judging them. A good teacher of religious education would have the same qualities as any other good teacher. Jean Holm summed them up as;

> the professional qualities of conscientiousness and integrity, sensitivity to other people and concern for the pupils, a real interest in the questions with which his subjects deals and a determination to acquire the knowledge needed to teach it. (Holm, 1975, pp. 5f)

She saw the new objective approach to the study of religion as liberating for children and teacher. No longer would children feel they were being 'got at' by a teacher aiming to convert them. Teachers could no longer be seen as simply teaching their own faith and needed to be trained in religious education as in any other subject. In the period from 1965 to 1977 over half of all RE teachers were unqualified in the subject (Sutcliffe, 1984, p. 339). There is no knowing how many of them had any religious faith.

The syllabuses of the 1970s and 1980s were influenced by the explicit approach. One of the earliest, and most notorious, of that type was the Birmingham Agreed Syllabus (1975), notorious because of the inclusion of 'non-religious stances for living', Communism, Marxism and Humanism for adolescents (Birmingham Education Committee, 1975, pp. 161ff). The format, now the usual one for syllabuses, was a short syllabus setting out the areas to be studied and a loose-leaf handbook with detailed courses and lists of resources for each age-group. Rather than being reserved for older children, courses on five world religions were set out for 12-16 year olds and included in all the themes for younger children. The objectives set out for the study of 'religious and non-religious stances for living' were that they should be; descriptive, objective, critical and experiential. The teacher should be committed to the value of studying religious experience and to 'the principle of fair mindedness'. The teacher is to engage in 'an objective, open-ended exploration' (Birmingham Education Committee, 1975, p. 25).

Through the phenomenological approach pupils could gain knowledge of world religions, and, what Jean Holm expressed as, 'understanding of what it would mean to take a religion seriously', developing empathy with the believer. In practice the approach had a number of problems including the sheer amount of information that could be put in a syllabus; the dangers of trivialising complex beliefs and practices and the practicality and desirability of maintaining an open, non-judgmental approach. However another impetus to that approach has been the view that teachers can promote tolerance between different ethnic groups in Britain (Meakin 1988, p. 95, Department of Education and Science, 1989a, section 8).

At its worst the approach could lead to a superficial overview of a wide range of beliefs from animism to Bah'ai, taught by teachers' without the benefit of any academic study of non-Christian religions. An objective approach could lead to the view that it did not matter what anyone believed, rather than inviting pupils to take religion seriously. While earlier approaches encouraged the pupil to find a faith to live by, and thus make personal judgements on the validity of different religions, the phenomenological approach required a suspension of judgement. The approach was therefore disliked by those who wanted Christianity to have a special place in religious education. The introduction of the 1988 Education Reform Bill provided an opportunity for those who wanted to re-Christianise RE, to restore the subject 'to its original integrity' (Baroness Cox, Hansard, House of Lords, 1988, vol. 496, c. 505). The next chapter looks at the debate surrounding the 1988 Education Reform Bill and the effects of the legislation on religion in education.

3 Religion in education from 1988

> the study and practice of Christianity in our schools will tend to curb
> evil and promote the good. That is what we need. (Lord Chateris,
> 1988, Hansard, House of Lords, vol. 496, c. 510)

The extended debate on the religious clauses of the Education Reform Bill
occupied 370 hours of Parliamentary debate and references to religious
education filled about fifteen pages altogether in the final draft compared
with a few lines when the Bill was first published (Church Times, 26.8.88).
The revival of attention to religious education revealed deeply felt concerns
about the nature of society and its shared values with differing views as to
the roles of schools, homes and churches. These concerns have continued
to be expressed by religious leaders, politicians and educationalists and
debated in the media. The purpose of this chapter is briefly to consider the
debate on the Education Reform Bill and the effect of the new legislation
on religion in schools.

Debate on the Education Reform Bill

The main purpose of the Education Reform Bill was to introduce a National
Curriculum for schools and the Government had plainly felt that no
particular attention needed to be given to religious education or assemblies
when drawing up the proposals. They were already required by law and the
Government did not see any necessity to make the law more specific. The
concern of the National Curriculum was to emphasise the importance of
those subjects seen as crucial for economic development, particularly
science and technology. Throughout the debate on the religious clauses of
the Education Reform Bill three strands of thought could be detected, those
of the Government, the traditionalists and the Labour multi-culturalists.
The view of the traditionalists in both Lords and Commons was that
religious education would be neglected at society's peril.   Through

Christian worship and the teaching of Christian beliefs and values children are said to learn the basis of British culture and individual morality. A group of Conservative peers was incensed by the drift away from Christian values in industrial society. The new curriculum with its emphasis on the economic needs of society was in danger of losing any moral basis. The view that Christian education is necessary in schools in order to teach society's basic values is not one generally shared by other countries. In the United States of America the public school system aims to instil moral values without any religious education and in France it is explicitly excluded from State schools. The third group, led by the Labour shadow education spokesman Jack Straw, resisted attempts to 'Christianise' religious education in schools. For them, religious education in its multi-faith form is a useful tool in modern pluralist society to teach tolerance and community values. Under current legislation schools were able to plan their own religious education and assemblies in such a way as to avoid many children having to 'opt out'.

The debate in both Houses of Parliament, and in the press, on the religious clauses of the Education Reform Bill centred on a dispute between those who argued for Christian education and worship, making the 1944 Education Act provisions more explicit, and those who felt there was merit in the status quo, in some cases only because it was recognised that in England there must be some religious teaching in schools. The supporters of Christian religious education tended to be critical of multi-faith approaches and of religiously uncommitted teachers. They saw an important role for religious education in instilling personal morality. Christian beliefs and worship were seen as the underpinning of British history and culture. The stress was on moral values and 'religious conviction' so that supporters included Roman Catholic members and the Chief Rabbi as well as Protestants. Those opposed to a greater emphasis on Christianity also saw a role for religious education in teaching moral values, but not in the sense of 'making them good' on an individual basis. They emphasised the role of modern multi-cultural approaches in helping children to be tolerant in a pluralist society. For them the attempts to 'Christianise' religious education would lead to problems of indoctrination and intolerance.

Those supporting Christian religious education in both Houses of Parliament expected a great deal of schools in terms of correcting behaviour by instilling moral values. The religious and moral education link was expressed with varying degrees of subtlety in the debate on the Reform Bill. Some members of Parliament saw religious education as acting in a straightforward, direct way to improve standards of behaviour in society and ensure that children know the difference between right and wrong. The Chief Rabbi, in the House of Lords, thought 'particular attention should be given to the moral dimension in preparing the rising generation for responsible marriage and responsible citizenship' (Lord Jakobovits, 3.5.88, Hansard, House of Lords, vol. 496, c. 420). Mr. Harry Greenway, who had been a schoolteacher, commented;

> never has there been a greater need for an assertion, an improvement and re-establishment of religious education in schools. There is considerable violence not only at football matches but in many other areas. One in three of the population is convicted of a criminal offence by the age of 28. Families are under great stress with the breakdown of one in three marriages. (23.3.88, Hansard, no. 130, c. 416)

Another Conservative member, Anthony Coombs, used statistics on truancy rates and attacks on teachers and the attitudes of the young to vandalism, to argue that 'we have a society that is looking for a spiritual and moral lead' to which 'Christian based religious education' could contribute (Hansard, no. 130, c. 403). Sir Rhodes Boyson (Conservative), former Minister of State for Education and an ex-headmaster, emphasised moral teaching through religious education in classrooms and assembly 'that suffuses much of the rest of the curriculum' (Hansard, no. 130, c. 411).

From this perspective the importance of religious education lies in the values it imparts and which underlie all aspects of school life. It is not one subject among many but, as the Roman Catholic Bishop Konstant put it, 'the very kernel of the curriculum, the foundation of an entire educational process, the core of the core curriculum' (Catholic Herald, 15.4.88, p. 3). The values it imparts will benefit the individual and society. On the individual level anti-social behaviour could be reduced through moral teaching and religious education can develop the child in ways left untouched by teaching knowledge and training children for careers (Boyson, 23.3.88, Hansard, vol. 130, c. 413). On the level of society a lack of moral education can lead to instability; 'broken homes cost the nation far more, socially and economically, than AIDS' (Jackobovits, 3.5.88, Hansard, House of Lords, vol. 496, c. 420). The assumption running through these comments is that morality can and should be taught through religion. Lord St. John of Fawsley (Conservative) explicitly stated that 'history affords no example of a society which has permanently maintained morality without a religious basis ... no religion, no morality' (Hansard, House of Lords, vol. 496, c. 417f). The President of the Prayer Book Society, Lord Charteris, stated his certainty 'that the study and practice of Christianity in our schools will tend to curb evil and promote the good. That is what we need' (Hansard, House of Lords, vol. 496, c. 510). Speaking at meetings of the General Synod of the Church of England, on separate occasions, the Home Secretary and the Secretary of State for Education both stressed the role of the Church in imparting moral values, particularly to the young (Church Times, 10.2.89, p. 12, The Times, 11.2.88). Another Conservative MP, Mr. Graham Riddick, criticised Church leaders for failing to provide strong moral leadership (10.3.89, Hansard, vol. 148, c. 1139).

'Practice' in the form of Christian worship was seen as an integral part of Christian education by Baroness Cox and her supporters. Such worship was not to be confused with 'a celebration of shared values' (12.5.88, Hansard, House of Lords, vol. 496,c. 1345). They did not want to draw a sharp distinction between worship whether it takes place in school, Church, home or the House of Lords itself. 'If we are Christians give us Christian worship' (c. 1350). However, the Bishop of London (Graham Leonard) saw difficulties in achieving Christian worship. It would not become Christian 'just by passing a few words in a Bill' (12.5.88, Hansard, House of Lords, vol. 496, c. 1351).

Underlying the preceding discussion is a Durkheimian view of strong moral rules as the key to social order. For the speakers, as for Durkheim, morality to be effective must have a 'sacred quality', here identified with conventional religion particularly Christianity (Durkheim, 1915, 415). The necessary connection of morality and religion was questioned by Lord Houghton (Labour) who asked; 'Must we teach them religion in order to achieve some concept of morality, human relationship, affection and understanding?' to which, according to Hansard, the Lords replied 'yes' (3.5.88, Hansard, House of Lords, vol. 496, c. 423). Other members of both Houses used examples where religious belief brought conflict and social problems, particularly in Northern Ireland and the Middle East. These members stressed the problems of divisions and intolerance between those of different beliefs and the need to consider the changed religious situation in Britain, since the 1944 Education Act with the presence of significant numbers of people from non-Christian religions and a variety of cultures. The Guardian reported that 'some clerics, even within the Church of England, were horrified by the tone of much of the debate in the House of Lords which appeared to be dominated by the belief that Christianity had the monopoly of moral virtue' (Guardian, 28.6.88, p. 21).

Multi-faith teaching

Those who did emphasise the link between morality and religion also tended to criticise modern multi-faith approaches in religious education. Since the 1970s religious education syllabuses have stressed knowledge and understanding of religion rather than commitment to Christian values. In this sense modern religious education does not appeal to those who expect it to 'curb evil and promote good'. The values particularly conveyed in recent syllabuses are tolerance and understanding of other peoples' beliefs and customs. Religious education is justified on educational grounds. The British Journal of Religious Education, supporting that view in an editorial commenting on the Education Reform Bill, said that the 'Christianising amendments';

> which thrust Christianity into a position of embarrassing prominence, are contrary to the British tradition, are not easily compatible with educational principles ... and seem unlikely to promote a society in which sympathetic acceptance and mutual understanding mark the relations between different religions and communities. (British Journal of Religious Education, vol. 11, no. 1, p. 2)

Baroness Cox criticised the multi-faith approach as confusing and superficial and cited GCSE syllabuses, various agreed syllabuses and specific teaching materials, saying that 'increasingly teachers are feeling the pressure in certain local authorities to play down Christianity and to teach a multi-faith curriculum' (Hansard, House of Lords, vol. 496, c. 503). In the foreword to a booklet by two teachers on the current state of religious education and worship she wrote;

> Many of our children are in schools where they are denied the experience of religious worship at all, and where teaching about Christianity has either been diluted to a multi-faith relativism or has become little more than a secularised discussion of social and political issues. These developments violate both the letter and the spirit of the law [i.e. the 1944 Education Act]. (Baroness Cox, Burn and Hart, 1988)

Lord Jacobovits, then Chief Rabbi, quoted with approval, Rabbi Jonathan Sacks' description of the consequences of teaching children about every religion with which they might have contact;

> a touch of Christianity; a dash of Judaism; a slice of Islam; and so on through a fruit cocktail of world faiths ... In trying to teach all faiths it is possible that we succeed in teaching none. (Hansard, House of Lords, vol. 496, c. 420)

Religious education teachers

For those opposing the comparative religion approach the religious educators in schools should be teachers who themselves have faith. Rhodes Boyson, in the House of Commons, stated that 'There must be faith. Those who teach religious education must believe in it' (23.3.88, Hansard, vol. 130, c. 413). Baroness Cox argued that 'many Christian teachers now feel unable to teach the new style religious education because it betrays the integrity of their faith' but 'many of them would be willing to teach again with the definition of religious education' contained in the amendments to the Education Reform Bill (Hansard, House of Lords, vol. 496,c. 504f). The Chief Rabbi also stressed the importance of teachers being able to transmit 'a commitment even more than mere knowledge. A religiously indifferent teacher can hardly instil religious convictions and sensitivities' (ibid, c. 419). The Archbishop of Canterbury, in the House of Lords, argued that 'the Churches must recruit and give opportunities for training and retraining teachers who are serious about their own faith' (ibid, c. 511). At the launching of religious education guidelines for Church schools in the Diocese of London (2.12.88), the Bishop urged parish clergy 'to encourage young people to enter the teaching profession' (Church Times, 9.12.88). The Association of Christian teachers had, some months before, argued that those who train and appoint religious education teachers can 'no longer afford 'the deep suspicion' they have often harboured towards committed Evangelical Christians' (Church Times, 3.6.88). Whereas the early religious education syllabuses assumed that teachers would be Christians, now they were expected to be committed to a faith rather than 'religiously indifferent'.

Given the numbers of teachers involved in religious education, particularly non-specialists in primary schools, it would be clearly unrealistic to hope that they would all be committed to any religion, although that would depend on the definition of 'commitment'. General belief in God can still be assumed to be widespread, but a more rigorous definition involving regular worship would exclude many in Church aided schools as well as in ordinary state schools (discussed in chapter 4 on church schools).

The strengthening of Christian teaching in schools was assumed by its supporters to have the backing of parents, particularly the 'vast majority' who would say they are Christian but do not go to Church. 'Most of those people do not feel capable of teaching Christianity to their children and rely on the schools to do the job properly' (Lord Swinfen) (Hansard, House of Lords, 3.5.88, vol. 496, c. 516). Lord Thorneycroft argued that a way must be found to 'give Christian education properly in our schools' and so 'produce the results which millions of parents are asking for' (Hansard, House of Lords, 5.5.88, vol. 496, c. 777). Those opposed to the Christianising amendments did not dispute that parental support. However, they argued the need for safeguards for those of other religions and none and asked why the schools should be expected, as Lord Peston put it, to 'make up the deficiency of the home in religion' (Hansard, House of Lords, 3.5.88, vol. 496, c. 510). The picture of society as consisting of small numbers having a particular religion and large numbers of nominal Christians, who would often identify themselves as Church of England, was largely borne out by the evidence contained in chapter 2. However nominally Christian parents do not necessarily support religious education and assemblies because they want their children to 'be brought up as Christians in schools' and expect it to 'lead to good behaviour', as Lord Charteris assumed (Hansard, House of Lords, 3.5.88, vol. 496, c. 510) Both the assumption that religious education is moral education and that parents want Christian education rather than a multi-faith approach were examined in the case study of three Cornish schools in chapter 6.

'Non-Christian' faiths

In both the Houses of Parliament, there were continual references to non-Christian faiths in the debate on the Education Reform Bill. Those members in favour of Christian education stressed the support received from other faiths and from black Christians, thus avoiding charges of racism. Lord Thorneycroft, in supporting Baroness Cox's amendments, referred to the Chief Rabbi's support and to an incident referred to by Baroness Cox in which an iman prayed in a mosque 'that the name of Christ would once again be revered in British schools' (Hansard, House of Lords, 3.5.88, vol. 496, c. 504). Those arguing for the 'Christianising' amendments to the Bill referred to support from members of other faiths, particularly Jews and Muslims, who, as Bishop Graham Leonard stated, wish religion to be taken seriously and for this reason may send their children to Church of England schools (Hansard, House of Lords, 3.5.88, vol. 496, c. 507).

Lord Thorneycroft picked these comments up and argued;

> with the West Indians clamouring for it, with the Moslems praying for it, and with the Jews urging it in this House, what case is there for not having Christian education in the schools? (Hansard, House of Lords, 3.5.88, vol. 496, c. 514)

Baroness Cox recognised that support for multi-faith teaching might arise from a respect for non-Christians but argued that this was misguided because 'representatives of other faiths ... emphasise that they do not wish us to destroy our Christian birthright in this way' (Hansard, House of Lords, 3.5.88, vol. 496, c. 503). In the House of Commons the shadow education spokesman, Jack Straw, criticised those seeking to include a requirement that teaching and worship should be Christian arguing that the debate raised;

> profound issues of tolerance and questions about how we treat people who have different faiths from our own. (Hansard, 18.7.88, vol. 137, c. 810)

Nigel Spearing (Labour), also supporting the less specific wording of the 1944 Education Act on religion in schools stressed the importance of schools inculcating tolerance even if this is not widespread in society at large. In 'multi-cultural, multi-racial and multi-religious areas' headteachers are 'battling to try to create corporate tolerance in a sea of religious and social problems' (Hansard, 18.7.88, vol. 137, c. 829).

Religious education post 1988

Under the 1988 Education Reform Act Religious Education became part of the 'basic curriculum' together with the core and foundation subjects of the National Curriculum (Education Reform Act, 1988, p. 2040). Any agreed syllabus 'shall reflect the fact that the religious traditions in Great Britain are in the main Christian whilst taking account of the teaching and practices of the other principal religions are presented in Great Britain' (Education Reform Act, 1988, p. 2044). In the 1944 Act the character of 'collective worship' was not specified except that it should not 'be distinctive of any particular denomination' in a county school (Education Act 1944, section 26). In the 1988 Act worship in county schools was 'in the main, to reflect the broad traditions of Christian belief in ways appropriate to the age, aptitude and family background of the pupils involved' though it was not to be 'distinctive of any particular Christian denomination' (Department of Education and Science, 1989b). There was still provision for parents to withdraw their children from assembly, as there was under the 1944 Education Act. Standing Advisory Councils were to be set up by each L.E.A. to advise the authority on Religious Education, including collective worship and they would be able to call for a review of the local agreed syllabus (Education Reform Act, 1988, p. 2044). Agreed syllabuses were still to be drawn up by a conference appointed by each Local Education Authority. The conferences would consist of four groups representing the Local Education Authority, teachers' associations, the Church of England and 'Christian and other religious denominations' which 'appropriately reflect the principal traditions in the area' (Education Reform Act, 1988, p. 2046). Headteachers of county schools could, after consultation with their governors, ask the SACRE (Standing Advisory Council for Religious Education) to lift the requirement for Christian collective worship for their school or for certain pupils. Such an exemption would last for five years before another application was required. By February 1990 about 250 schools in England and Wales had applied to have the requirement for mainly Christian worship lifted (Independent on Sunday, 18.2.90).

The implementation of the National Curriculum and scheme of testing has begun to shape religious education syllabuses and programmes in school. Although religious education was part of the 'basic curriculum' under the 1988 provisions, the Secretary of State was not obliged to set out attainment targets or programmes of study and assessment, as he was for National Curriculum subjects. Religious education did not have a national syllabus unlike the other subjects. Those involved in religious education immediately saw that resources would be concentrated on the National Curriculum subjects and unless religious education adopted the same arrangements it would not have any chance of parity with those subjects (AREIA, 1989, p. 1). The Religious Education Council in a 'Handbook for Agreed Syllabus Conferences, SACREs and schools' argued that such bodies 'may decide that it is in the interests of religious education and will enhance its status if it takes on board comparable approaches' (Religious Education Council, 1989, p. 15). Thus various interested organizations have published the 'attainment targets', 'programmes of study' and 'assessment arrangements' for religious education which are required of other National Curriculum subjects. The agreed syllabuses and handbooks written since the 1988 Act specify attainment targets related to the key stages of the National Curriculum and use the new key words of attitudes and skills which should be achieved by children at each key stage (Howarth, 1993).

Cornwall County Agreed Syllabus and Handbook 1989

In 1979 Cornwall county was still showing a sturdy independence from other areas of the country. In other areas non-Christian religions had originally been introduced into syllabuses because members of those religions lived there. Only later was it seen as worthwhile for all children to learn about 'other faiths'. This change in educational thinking rather than any increase in the non-Christian population in the area accounted for the difference between the 1979 and 1989 syllabuses. In 1979 world religions were not included in the syllabus for infants or juniors because in the area 'our culture is still basically Christian' . They were included ten years later and said to be 'all the more significant an element in the whole life experience of [local] children' because of their 'lack of first hand experience' of a multi-faith society. The aims and objectives were more detailed and, although some of the themes were the same as in 1979 the approach was no longer from a Christian perspective and a variety of religions were included in all the examples. For example the topic on 'Friends' (1979) and 'Friends and neighbours' (1989) is, in both syllabuses, aimed at infant age children. In 1979 the note for the teacher assumed a religious basis for the values and attitudes which the topic aimed to develop;

> When small children come to school they find that they are members of a much larger community than that of the family and they need

help in learning to progress from an egocentric view of life and to learn something of the joy of people's love and care of each other. They need to learn that Jesus was and still is the friend of everyone. John 14 v.15 John 15 v.12 (1979, Infant section, p. 12)

In 1989 the overall aim was 'to develop sensitivity and tolerance' and the objectives were now;

1. Empathy for other people and their experiences.

2. Awareness and understanding of themselves, displaying a positive attitude to their emotions

Organised religion was no longer the mainspring for the theme although one aspect of the topic was 'Friends in the Bible' and Biblical references were listed first under resources.

The approach advocated as 'essential' was an open one, although it was recognised that 'there is still opposition' to that approach in the county. Non-religious responses to life, which when included in the Birmingham syllabus and handbook of 1975 caused controversy, were said to be raised inevitably when dealing with areas of beliefs and doctrines.

The syllabus combined implicit and explicit elements in the four areas of concern it outlined. These covered the development of, 'understanding and insight' into religions, with Christianity occupying the largest amount of time; the pupils' 'own personal search for meaning'; 'insight into the experiential dimension of religion' and 'a capacity for tolerance and empathy' (1989, p. 7). There was a section on evaluation which acknowledged that schools might want to use the same form of evaluation as National Curriculum subjects to maintain parity with other academic subjects (1989, p. 22). These would no doubt have been specified if the syllabus had been wholly written after the 1988 Act. Cornwall LEA took part in the 'Forms of Assessment in Religious Education' (FARE) project which was engaged in working out forms of assessment for religious education (Copley, Priestley et al, 1991).

Assessment in Religious Education

A survey of teams of south west teachers taking part in the FARE project, found reservations about their ability, or willingness, to assess implicit religious education but no objection to the testing of explicit material in the form of factual knowledge (Copley, Priestley et al, 1990, p. 28). The interim report from FARE suggested methods of assessment which involve self-assessment by the pupil as being more appropriate to the elements of awareness and personal response, for example, profiles negotiated between

42

pupil and teacher, diaries, open-ended discussion and creative work. The report proposed six 'Attainment Targets' which should be 'present and given equal weight' throughout a religious education curriculum; these were;

Awareness of mystery
Questions of meaning
Values and commitments
Religious belief
Religious practice
Religious language (Copley, Priestley et al, 1990, p. 29).

There was nothing particularly new in the content of the suggested programmes of study but they were set out in accordance with the new terminology of Key Stages and Statements of Attainment (SATs). These set out what pupils 'should know' or 'should be aware' of, and what they should be able to do to show this knowledge or awareness; whether in writing, talking or explaining to someone else, drama, movement, art or model making (Copley, Priestley et al, 1990, pp. 32-65). Such a variety of types of assessment allowed for implicit religious education to be assessed. An example from Key Stage 3 and Attainment Target one (Awareness of Mystery) Statement of Attainment 4 read;

Pupils should be aware of their own feelings relating to the exploration of religion and life-experience in such a way that they can maintain a personal record of these, and, as long as privacy is not invaded, share these with another person or group. (Copley and Priestley, 1990, p. 49)

The final report in 1991 included specific examples of assessment used by teachers in the south west (Copley, Priestley et al, 1991). The use of the current terminology of assessment will presumably allow religious education to be presented in the same way as other National Curriculum subjects in the reports for parents, which are now compulsory. Since parents will have a variety of religious and non-religious commitments the reporting of children's assessment scores could lead to misunderstandings unless parents know what is being measured and make the distinction between attainment in religious education and attainment of religious faith and practice.

The introduction to the final report stated that the aim of religious education was giving pupils an 'understanding of the present world ... so that they are in a position to make choices' (Copley, Priestley et al, 1991, p. 7). Whereas earlier discussions of religious education would have stressed the need to avoid indoctrination of pupils, the main barrier to pupils making choices now was said to be 'sheer ignorance'. The pen portraits given in the final report illustrated the central values of religious education. Those pupils, of all ages, considered 'less than average' shared certain characteristics. They were said not to listen to other peoples' opinions, to be insensitive to others' beliefs and feelings, to show 'little empathy' and to be unable to share and discuss ideas (Copley, Priestley et al, 1991, pp. 300-307).

Cornwall Agreed Syllabus 1995 to 2000

The most recent syllabus for Cornwall is based on the national model agreed syllabuses produced by the Schools Curriculum and Assessment Authority (SCAA) in 1994. It illustrates the greater uniformity following on from the 1988 reforms. Local flavour occurs only in the mention of Cornish Saints and in the example of a policy on collective worship in a county school;

> *Any* school is a county school, serving a [space] community in an almost totally and mostly nominal Christian area of the south west of England. (Cornwall SACRE, 1995, p. 13)

The policy goes on to say that pupils will be prepared 'for life not only in their own community but in a wider world'.

Comment

Specific moral values are once more to the forefront of religious education programmes. After the brief period of an 'open' approach, multi-cultural religious education reasserted the importance of factual content but with the aim of conveying values of tolerance and empathy rather than of leading children to Christ. All recent syllabuses have shared a consensus on the importance of those values and included the variety of religions present in Britain. The 1989 Cornwall county syllabus was explicit in its aim of creating in pupils;

> a capacity for tolerance and empathy, to enable them to live with people of different ways of life, without feeling threatened; to remove sources of racial, religious and social conflict. (Cornwall Education Committee, 1989, p. 7)

Politicians in the debates on the 1988 Act still talked about 'right' and 'wrong' but the syllabuses stressed social values, aiming for communities which lived together peaceably rather than the leading of people to God. In that sense religious education in the 1990s again aims to instil society's values rather than be 'open-ended' but the values have changed as Britain is

44

seen to be 'multi-faith' rather than Christian. Parallels can be drawn between changes in religious education, changes in religiosity in Britain and in ideas about the role of Church schools. Until the 1960s, and later in Cornwall, syllabuses of religious education and Church schools were intended to produce children with knowledge of Christianity, to convince them of its truth and train them in Christian practice through school worship. By the 1990s caring, tolerance and a positive attitude to religion were goals shared by Church schools and religious education.

The high expectations pinned to religious education in the period immediately after the second world war were not fulfilled in any obvious sense, such as increasing church attendance or higher standards of morality. Changes in religious education continued to mirror changes in educational orthodoxy. Religious education was still seen, mainly by those outside teaching, as capable of curing societies' ills and making children good. Such a view would lead to a programme of Christian education in schools teaching individual morality derived from the Bible, as some taking part in the debate on the 1988 Act would have liked, perhaps with separate provision for those of different faiths. Despite the initial feelings that such a traditional view triumphed in the 1988 provisions for religious education, it appears that a multi-faith approach focusing on social morality is continuing to develop using the framework of the National Curriculum subjects.

Reactions to the Act

The debate over the amendments to the Act brought religious education and worship in schools to the attention of the churches, teachers and the general public. However there continues to be a division between the prevailing view in parliament, which demanded a more precise definition of religious education and worship, and the views of those actually be implementing the Act: headteachers, teachers and their advisors in Church and professional organizations. Straightforward Christian education was demanded by Baroness Cox and her supporters while professional educationalists were concerned to ensure that religious education was considered on a par with other subjects in the National Curriculum. The traditionalists saw both classroom religious education and school worship as vehicles for the transmission of Christian values, so did not particularly stress the development of RE as an academic subject. The consensus among the professionals was that religious education must aim at understanding rather than commitment and that specialist teachers using modern educational methods and resources were required as in any other subject. Thus while the government's attitude, expressed by the Secretary of State for Education was that the settlement represented 'a great opportunity which I hope the

Churches will now seize' (Hansard, 1988, vol. 130, c. 423). Reactions from the professionals were less favourable. Dr. Brian Gates, chairman of the Religious Education Council, 'regretted that the 1944 Act had been changed', according to an article in the Guardian newspaper (Guardian, 28.6.88). The editor of the British Journal of Religious Education also expressed doubts over the wisdom of the more precise definition of content in the new Act, 'in the long run Butler will prove to have been wiser than Baker in this respect' (British Journal of Religious Education, Spring 1989, pp. 61, 91). A survey of 234 secondary headteachers just before the requirements on worship came into force found 'only one, a Roman Catholic, [who] expressed enthusiasm for them', the others cited reasons including a lack of space for the whole school to meet and a lack of staff to take such a daily assembly (Church Times, 7.7.89). The National Association of Headteachers felt it necessary to issue forty-five pages of guidelines on religious education and worship and were particularly concerned over the possibility of increased withdrawals by parents and teachers from RE and worship because of the emphasis on Christianity, which would 'threaten the unity of the school' (Church Times, 3.3.89) . A diverse group of interested parties, including all those mentioned, the Association of Christian teachers and the Islamic Society for the Promotion of Religious Tolerance, shared a concern that the Act could affect relations between different religions in Britain (Church Times, 3.3.89, Guardian, 28.6.88, British Journal of Religious Education, Spring 1989). A circular from the Department for Education (January 1994) warned that the law on religious education and worship must be complied with in full and reinforced the view that Christianity should predominate. Collective worship 'must contain some elements which relate specifically to the traditions of the Christian belief and which accord a special status to Jesus Christ'. At the same time RE and worship should promote respect among pupils for different beliefs from their own and allow as many pupils as possible to participate.

Since then the National Association of Head Teachers members have continued to regard the rules on collective worship and religious education to be 'unacceptable and unworkable', including half the heads of church schools (Church Times, 3.6.94). Suggestions from within the churches have included fewer acts of worship of higher quality (Archbishop of York, on a different occasion, the Evangelical Alliance), pupils and teachers being able to 'opt out mentally' (Churches Joint Education Policy Committee) and spiritual rather than Christian assemblies (Bishop of Ripon) (Independent, 6.1.95; Church Times, 11.11.94, 16.12.94, 17.3.95). One development has been the withdrawal of Muslim children from religious education (but not worship) organised by Muslim action group in West Yorkshire. Their objections were reported to be to the prominence given to Christianity and to multi-faith RE which they felt confused children (Church Times, 26.1.96). Support for this view came from the pressure group Parental Alliance for Choice in Education who urged Christian parents to seek Christian RE for their children so 'this multi-faith, progressive education nonsense is blown sky-high' (Times, 6.2.96). In Birmingham a primary school with a 70 per cent Muslim intake provided separate Islamic religious education taught by a Muslim teacher using a syllabus agreed to by the local SACRE, City Council and parents (Times, 5.2.96). Predictably the traditionalists supported both parental choice and faith teaching whereas the Professional Council for Religious Education's representative said that parents were misunderstanding the nature of RE which is educational 'not about indoctrination or conversion'. However, the Muslim leaders had not necessarily misunderstood the nature of RE but rather they had understood it and preferred confessional Islamic teaching for their children.

While the various protagonists in this continuing debate realign themselves the position of the Church of England and its schools is ambiguous. As the established church which maintains a presence throughout the country it encompasses Anglo-Catholics and Evangelicals, some of whom would sympathise with the demand for faith teaching in schools, and a large body of nominal adherents who want some religion in school but nothing which smacks of indoctrination. The role of Anglican schools, amid the changes in culture, religion and education, is considered next.

4 Religion in church schools

Why did you choose to send your child to the Church of England school?

> Not because it's a church school but because it's only 5 minutes away ...
> Everyone said it's the best and you'll be lucky to get them in there ...
> They've got all the facilities there, playing fields - they've even got carpets in the corridors ...
> I'd not come across a church school before. It's a brand new school
> I thought a church school would be better. I hoped the discipline would be better ...

The mothers quoted above had children at a church aided school. One school was the village school, which for historical reasons was a voluntary aided Anglican school, the other school in Penvollard was newly built to provide an alternative to the existing county school, as explained in chapter 5. Children were sent to the village school as the local one whereas the facilities and reputation of Penvollard church school were factors as well as convenience. Only two mothers mentioned the church connection as a reason for their choice. This chapter discusses the aims of Church of England aided schools as expressed in official publications at national and diocesan level and through surveys of the views of governors and staff. Two issues arising from the mothers' comments are whether there is any justification for perceiving church schools in general as 'good' schools and how strong their Anglican identity should be according to those involved in running them.

Whilst religious education in schools has ceased to have the stated aim of making children Christian and non-Christian religions are a compulsory part of every agreed syllabus, around a quarter of pupils still attend an aided or controlled denominational school and nearly one in four primary schools in England are Church of England.[1] While Catholic schools offer the alternative of a Catholic education, Anglican schools may serve as the only primary education in a rural area or as the local school in an urban area in which most children have a faith other than Christianity. Thus there may be a tension for Anglican schools in maintaining their traditional dual role of providing education as a service to the whole community and teaching, or more recently, educating in, the Christian faith (Levitt, 1995a).

Catholic schools tend to have a stronger denominational identity than Anglican schools with the clear function of providing Catholic education for children from Catholic families; a lack of Catholic pupils thus provides an argument for closure, as in the case of the Birmingham sixth form college closing because the trustees felt it had too few Catholic students to comply with the Trust Deed (Church Times, 13.5.94). However, the Church of England as the established church serves, at least in theory, all those living in the parish not just the regular congregation. For those not committed to an alternative denomination or religion, the Church is still a resource to be called upon, if only for first marriages and funerals. The church school is also seen as a normal part of the educational provision to be used as required and is popular with parents who are largely absent from a church (Levitt, 1995b). Whereas parents would be unlikely to become Catholic in order to send their children to a Catholic school, the Church of England is more readily available to casual attenders and nominal Christians. Anglican schools are in the unique position of attracting large numbers of children from families who do not practice any religion but are not hostile to the church and want a service which it provides. What should be the aims of these schools?

The aims of Church of England schools: official publications

If the Christian faith has nothing to say or do in [our school communities] then it ought to be abandoned. (Duncan, 1990)

The official publications can all agree on Geoffrey Duncan's comment made in a 1990 National Society publication but the difficulty comes in specifying the 'something'. There are references to 'certain educational potentialities not necessarily found in schools of different kinds'; to 'the distinctive alternative'; 'offering something further' and to 'a religious basis to educational endeavour', 'a recognisably Christian education' (Durham Report, 1970, Gay, 1982, p. 16, Diocese of Sheffield, 1985, section A16, Blackburn Diocesan Board of Education, 1994). According to a Manchester Diocesan report, there should be an agreed foundation to education in a church school, based on the shared assumptions of the head, staff, governors, parents and parish priest. All concerned should 'set their priorities by a code of Christian values' (Diocese of Manchester, 1983, p. 7). It would seem unlikely that governors and teachers, never mind parents, could be expected to share Christian values but official publications tend to move between Christian values in a broad sense and a more specific definition. Thus Dr. Runcie, when Archbishop of Canterbury summed up the approach to education that can be called Christian with a broad definition;

> Manifesting concern for every individual, for the whole person, demonstrating forgiveness and acceptance and building up a caring community in the school. (Runcie, 1982)

However, these qualities of concern for the individual, tolerance and caring are general humanistic values; would any non-Church school disagree with them?

Religious education and worship in Church of England schools

It might be expected that religious education would be distinctive in a church school; however, controlled schools use the local Agreed Syllabus except for pupils whose parents request denominational teaching. [2] In an aided school religious education and worship should be in accordance with the Trust Deed and overseen by the school governors (National Society, 1989a, p. 4). In practice though, Diocesan publications adopt the aims of modern religious education; teaching children about non-Christian faiths particularly stressing tolerance and respect for faiths which are different from their own. Church schools are more likely actually to teach classroom religious education according to Ofsted reports, rather than allow the syllabus to gather dust on a shelf (Hull, 1994, p. 130).

Although official publications subscribe to the ideas of modern 'open' RE, specific guidelines on teaching content may be contradictory when joined to the requirement to be 'distinctive'. A Sheffield Diocesan Handbook advocated 'open' religious education taking place in the context of a Christian school;

> Religious education in school seeks to help children become aware of, and to understand, religion and what it means to be religious. It is concerned to deepen and enrich an openness and sensitivity to life, and to encourage a questioning response to experience, and so contribute to each pupil's own spiritual development. (Diocese of Sheffield, 1985, A1)

However, a few pages later it is stated that the Church school is 'A Christian community whose faith should be apparent to all. ... The child in a church school has the opportunity to experience a living religion through the community of the school' (Diocese of Sheffield, 1985, A18). If faith is not

51

expected of children, parents or staff it is not clear 'whose faith would be apparent to all'. The quotation illustrates the dilemma for those who wish to support modern multi-faith religious education, to nurture pupils' own faith and to do it in a school which is distinctively Christian.

All schools are required to have a daily act of worship under the 1988 Education Reform Act, as they have been since 1944, with a provision for separate acts of worship for age groups or other school groups. Voluntary aided schools are also allowed to worship in a Church on any special occasion, as the provisions in the 1944 Act still apply, and have the right to make assemblies denominational. The National Society's booklet on school worship under the 1988 Act simply states that 'worship in aided, special agreement and controlled schools is bound by the requirements of each school's Trust Deed, which specifies the tradition on which it is to be based' (National Society, 1989b, p. 6). However, Christian worship based on the model of the Anglican Church's services (assumed in older Trust deeds) does not fit easily with modern RE and denominational worship is not the everyday practice even in aided schools. Several Diocesan publications acknowledge the difficulties by using the phrase popularised by John Hull of 'bringing children to the threshold of worship' (for example, Truro Diocese, 1988, p. 11; Diocese of London, 1988, section B5.). A 1985 General Synod report appeared to support an absence of denominationalism by citing the 'denominational concern' of some church schools as responsible for the parallels drawn between requests for Muslim aided schools and the Church's wish to retain its schools (General Synod Board of Education, 1985). In a survey the year before fewer than half the Anglican aided schools had a majority of assemblies that were even explicitly Christian (Francis, 1984c). Only 10 per cent of Gloucestershire Anglican aided primary schools claimed that their assemblies were 'explicitly Christian and denominational' compared with 87 per cent of Roman Catholic schools in the county (Francis 1987, pp. 81f).

Church schools and the community

Another theme in official publications is to stress the service of the school to the community; this could be distinctive if it meant close links with the local church and its members but, more often, it is the local community as a whole which is referred to. Colin Alves, when General Secretary of the National Society, said that he saw church schools as a base for creating community and as therefore responding to the varied needs of the community (Panorama, BBC1, 17.12.87). In this view Church schools have a role to play in promoting good relations between those from different religions and culture within the area, relations based on tolerance, understanding and love (Diocese of London, 1988, section B1). Opponents of church schools would argue that non-denominational schools are better equipped to promote these aims.

The unanswered question is whether the church school should serve any community, even if that community might share values at variance with Christian values. 'Responding' to the community's needs seems to imply giving them what they want unless of course the school decides what the community's needs are. The stress is on the school being inclusive not exclusive, tolerant rather than dogmatic. However, a National Society publication also mentions Christian values in a narrower sense;

> The Church school, like the Church, should be concerned to serve the community and to do this with sensitivity and compassion. The school is not the place for narrow evangelism (the children are a captive audience) but the teachers should be aware of their responsibility to witness to the truths and values of the school's Christian foundation. (Duncan 1990, p. 12)

This neatly combines the dual role, service to the community and witness to the Christian faith but makes the false assumption that all teachers will be Christians (who can witness to the truths) and does not acknowledge any problem in witnessing to only one faith in the community while serving all.

The staff's view

If schools are to 'witness to the truths' of Christianity their Christian commitment would seem to be essential. Although such commitment might be assumed in the case of most headteachers of *aided* schools, it is doubtful if it could apply to every member of staff. Despite the Terms of Union which apply to all Church of England aided schools, schools do not necessarily request any form of Christian allegiance or sympathy when appointing staff. In the 1839 terms of union

> the Masters and Mistresses are to be members of the Church of England. (National Society, 1839)

In the 1990 version,

> consistent with the primary duty to appoint good teachers, the Governing Body shall endeavour to appoint practising members of the Church of England or practising members of Christian religious denominations with which the Church of England enjoys good relationships and ecumenical co-operation. (National Society, 1990)

53

Although Francis has found Christian affiliation and churchgoing to be at a much higher level among church school teachers than in the population as a whole, the same support has not been shown for Church teaching or practice. His findings suggest that only Christian values in a broad sense and knowledge about the Christian faith are uncontroversial but specifically Anglican activities received minority support (Francis, 1986b). Almost all the aided schoolteachers surveyed agreed the goals of providing 'an atmosphere of Christian community' and 'putting into practise Christian values' were important but regular communion services or confirmation preparation were only accepted by around a quarter of the sample (Francis, 1986b, pp. 89f). 'Putting into practise Christian values' seems quite a specific goal but it may be that people assume that their normal behaviour will be 'Christian' without their having to think about it. Osmond reports Gallop poll findings that over 90 per cent of professionals and teachers agreed that 'most of my actions in private life fit in with Christian morality' and 'most of my actions in public life fit in with Christian morality' but only half the sample claimed to consciously take the Christian perspective into account when speaking or acting (Osmond, 1993, p. 84).

The Governors' view

In aided schools the church has the right to appoint a majority of the governors and the power of all governors in the areas of curriculum and financial management has been extended. The same pattern of majority support only for general Christian values and occasional practise was found in a study of governors in aided Church of England primary schools in the Oxford diocese (Kay, 1988). Using attitude statements it was found that statements like; 'aided schools should encourage Christian standards of behaviour' and 'Children in a Church of England aided school should be taught about Christian beliefs and practices', were uncontroversial, with less than one per cent disagreeing (Kay, 1988,p. 7). Ninety four per cent agreed that 'an aided school should have strong links with the local church and its congregation' but for most governors this did not mean that parish clergy should take part in class teaching 'at least once a fortnight' or that 'the local incumbent should be chairman of the governors of an aided school in his parish'. 'Strong links' seemed in practical terms to mean, for the majority, parish clergy conducting assemblies at least three or four times a term' and the school attending a church service at least once a year (Kay, 1988, pp. 7-11).

The opinions of the governors and teachers neatly illustrate the advantage of vague general statements on Church schools. Once the statements become more specific the divisions become apparent.

Church schools are often seen as places in which traditional values and teaching methods are perpetuated. Church schools may appear as 'safe' schools which 'exhibit features which are commonly associated with a good education - formal teaching, homework, school uniform, orderly conduct' (Gay, 1982, p. 42). An Oxford Diocesan report concludes that generally in Anglican schools as opposed to Roman Catholic ones ;

> The religious factor has neither been dominant enough in the life of the school nor crucial enough in the priorities of the parents to be an overriding consideration. (Gay, 1982, p. 27)

Parents, whether Anglicans or those whom the report calls 'passive agnostics', will decide for or against a church school for their children on a 'variety of criteria' rustling up the religious credentials if they want a particular school. In Penvollard teachers at church and county schools and some governors were aware of the reasons for the popularity of the church school. Asked why church schools are so popular in the diocese, a member of the diocesan education team replied; 'uniform, discipline, traditional education and manners'.

The dilemma for Church schools is that, in areas where there is a choice, they attract articulate parents by their reputation as providers of traditional education. If they become oversubscribed then they will tend to be unintentionally socially selective; probably the main reason for the high performance of Anglican comprehensive schools in the 'league tables' (O'Keefe, 1986, p. 63) Looking at the published GCSE league tables there are examples of Church schools which outperform all the other local schools by a large margin (e.g. Exeter); these schools are likely to be oversubscribed, and therefore operate admissions policies which tend, unintentionally, to lead to a socially skewed intake.   In some areas the intake will also be racially skewed. The unintentional social selection is illustrated by Penvollard Church school (page 85)

Although parents are primarily attracted by the social and academic reputation of church schools, this includes the general Christian ethos, with values of caring and a 'feeling of family' which fit in well with mainstream societal values. If schools attract parents because they are good schools, should they be content to serve the community in that way?. In the view of the World Council of Churches, mission, including the provision of schools,

> must be offered with no strings attached. It must not be a carrot to attract people to convert to Christianity. (Duncan, 1990, p. 8)

The nominal Christian using an Anglican school because it is a good school does not expect it to convert their child and the low key approach of most Anglican schools provides the elements of religion which are acceptable to the majority. The reaction of nominal Christian parents to Penvollard church school illustrates what is and is not acceptable to parents (see chapter 6).

Grant-maintained status

The provisions of the 1988 Education Reform Act for schools to 'opt out' of local government control has been taken up by fewer than 400 schools and both the Roman Catholic and Anglican churches have expressed reservations. Initially, Anglican comments stressed 'the effects of their actions on the rest of the maintained system in their area' particularly on the poorest and most deprived areas of the country (National Society, 1988). Catholic reports stressed administrative problems for the diocese and problems with the links between local church, school and Bishop. The Bishop had a duty to ensure a Catholic education for the Catholic children in his diocese but no say in whether a school should have grant maintained status (Catholic Herald, 19.2.88, p. 1; 15.4.88, p. 3). Both denominations opposed Government proposals for a 'fast-track' to grant-maintained status for all aided schools and the idea was abandoned by the Government a few months later (Times, 3.11.95; Church Times, 12.1.96). The opportunity for schools to develop distinctive identities is presented as a matter of parental choice, although the popular schools will be choosing rather than the parents. There are only 200 Anglican schools for secondary age children, where most selection takes place at present, but any form of selection will tend to have social consequences and (Anglican) religious criteria can be met by the more confident and determined parents rather than the more actively religious (see chapter 6).

Another possible development would be the granting of aided status for schools of faiths other than Christianity and Judaism. Although the Islamic Muslim school in Brent was refused aided status in 1993 after a ten year campaign there are likely to be further applications which the Education secretary has 'promised to consider' (Independent on Sunday, 25.9.94; Times, 17.1.96). There are around 30 Muslim schools in the UK which, if aided status was granted, would be likely to take on the Catholic rather than the Anglican model and be schools for children from the particular faith, perhaps attracting other families if they had spare places. The new Christian, evangelical, schools can also apply to opt in, though some would be too small or not prepared to teach the National Curriculum. Walford's research also indicated that headteachers were concerned that they would lose autonomy and many schools were in any case opposed to legislation which allowed the possibility of 'other faith' schools (Poyntz and Walford, 1994). One such school has applied and been rejected. In urban and suburban areas there may in the future be a variety of specialist and sectarian schools but in rural and less populated areas there will continue to be a local primary, often an Anglican school, and one secondary school.

The future

Popular with parents, successful in the league tables and not threatened by any of the main political parties, why should the future of aided and controlled schools be anything other than rosy? There is agreement among the Church and dioceses, governors and teachers that Anglican schools should encourage respect and tolerance towards each other's beliefs, be distinctively Christian with a high quality of religious education and worship, be caring communities in themselves and serve the community in which they are situated. However, any primary school considered 'good' would provide religious education and worship (to comply with the law), good pastoral care, strong links with the community and even what could be described as a Christian ethos, if this is used in the general sense of care and concern for others. Attempts to be more specific leads to contradictions in Church reports and divisions among those directly involved (including parents if there is any suspicion of evangelism/indoctrination).

Adrian Thatcher considers the same problem in relation to Church of England colleges; how can they be distinctive? He argues that four areas which have been suggested ; the chapel and chaplain, care for students, the Christian context and links with the community; are necessary but not sufficient to answer the question, 'What do voluntary colleges provide that the state sector does not? (Thatcher, 1990, pp. 168ff). For Thatcher a Church college should be distinctive by its curriculum which would provide a 'critical value-laden analysis' of society from the Christian tradition (Thatcher, 1990, p. 171). Given current methods of teaching children, the lack of staff informed and committed to a Christian tradition and the feelings of teachers and parents about indoctrination, it seems unlikely that a primary school could deliver such a curriculum, although it has been said that they do. The Chairman of the General Synod's Board of Education, David Young, wrote;

> the whole curriculum is coloured by this [Christian] perspective ...
> The church aided school takes the Christian story to be true, and
> offers it as a perspective for the interpretation of our world and our
> experience. (Young, 1995)

If church aided Anglican schools are more than their trust deeds and headteachers then they cannot be said to 'take the Christian story as true'. Some aided schools strive to appoint practising Christian staff but there are difficulties in finding committed Christians even for the senior posts (Church Times 26.1.96). If a more general Christian belief is meant then this would be unlikely to influence the world view or the curriculum as a whole. As discussed in chapter 6, many people claim to be Christian without expecting this to influence their daily life, work or moral decision-making (Osmond 1993).

Perhaps a more realistic model for Anglican church schools is a more woolly one. What might be seen as the weakness of Anglican schools; their ambivalence over having a clear Christian identity because of a desire to be tolerant and serve the whole community; can be seen as their strength. Parents may not send their children to an aided school because it is their local school, or, may choose it for a variety of social and educational reasons. The association of church schools with traditional education, discipline and perhaps social selection may not be the chosen image of clergy but it enables the Anglican church to maintain some contact with significant numbers of young children. However slight the influence on the children who attend them, this contact is important because with the decline in churchgoing it may be the most significant, or the only, contact which the Church and clergy will have with young families. At the same time church schools give the Church a legitimate voice in educational debate as provider of one in four primary schools in England.

Notes

1. Church of England primary schools form are well represented in rural areas; Catholic schools are on average larger and a higher proportion are secondary schools. Almost all Catholic schools are aided schools, there is one controlled school, whereas most Anglican schools opted for controlled status after the 1944 Education Act. Voluntary aided schools are schools provided and maintained by a voluntary body with the assistance of grant aid from central government for external repairs and improvements. Currently there are Church of England, Roman Catholic, Methodist and Jewish schools with aided status, including 25 Anglican-Methodist joint aided primary schools and six Anglican-Roman Catholic aided schools. Government grants of 85 per cent are available for the capital costs of new aided schools under conditions specified in section 13 of the 1980 Education Act . The local education authority are responsible for day to day running costs of aided schools including teachers' salaries and interior repairs. The churches' share in capital costs and external maintenance has been gradually decreased

from 50/50 with the State under the 1944 Education Act to only 15 per cent now. The Church does not provide any finance for the day-to-day running or maintenance of controlled schools but still has the right to appoint one-third of the governors . In aided schools the voluntary body may appoint a majority of the school governors. Aided schools may provide denominational religious instruction and worship. There are around 130 grant-maintained Anglican schools which are fully funded by the state and controlled by their governing bodies (Church Times, 6.10.95)

2. Controlled schools follow the local Agreed Syllabus except for pupils whose parents request denominational teaching, for which schools with more than two teachers may appoint 'reserved teachers' in proportion to the size of the staff. It is likely that few schools have withdrawal classes and in a survey of 44 controlled schools with at least three teachers only nine had appointed a reserved teacher (Francis, 1987, p. 92).

5 Religion in a community

Penvollard is one small town in a rural county which might be thought to be relatively unaffected by changes in the religious map elsewhere. There are few members of faiths other than Christianity, there are no religious buildings belonging to non-Christian faiths and the newest school is a Church of England aided primary school which is oversubscribed. Many of the activities for children have a connection with a church or are Christian in ethos. Nevertheless, the trends in religiosity which have been identified in previous chapters have been illustrated by comments from people in this Cornish community. Before looking in more detail at their views in chapter 6 these comments are put in context by a description of changes in the economy, population, religious life and schools of Penvollard. The empirical research was carried out from 1985 to 1992, although more recent data is quoted in some cases.

Cornwall: Economy and population

In Cornwall as a whole the population rose by a third from the 1960s to the late 1980s because of migration into the area and is still increasing. Although the county attracted older people seeking retirement homes, 70 per cent of incomers since the 1960s have been under 55 years old (Perry 1988, pp.34f). Eighteen year olds going on to higher education have usually had to leave the county (one in six did so in the 1980s). In the 1980s the population might be seen as consisting of three groups; local Cornish people who had never left the area (40-45 per cent), 'new settlers' who had moved in since the early 1960s (40-45 per cent) and 'returned exiles' (Perry, 1988, p.42). Each group tended to have a different employment profile. The 'locals' had lower qualifications, were less likely to own their own homes and more likely to work in lower paid, lower skilled jobs. The 'new settlers' tended to have the better paid and more skilled jobs in industry, commerce, local government, education and social services as well as being over represented among the 'entrepreneurs' starting new businesses. Those returning to Cornwall tended to occupy a middle position in terms of qualifications and employment .

Due to the influx of people into the east of the county the population was evenly divided between east and west Cornwall by the end of the 1980s. From being an economy based on the exploitation of natural resources, with copper, tin, arsenic mines, fishing, farming and ship repairs, Cornwall had come to depend significantly on the physical attractiveness of the area for new small businesses and tourists. In 1993 more than half the total employees were female and nearly 36 per cent of employees worked part time (Plymouth Business School 1995). Wages are below the national average .

Politically Cornwall has been distinctive for the relative strength of the Liberal party, and later the Liberal Democrats. In the 1992 General Election Liberal Democrats retained Truro, gained North Cornwall which they had lost to Conservatives in 1979 and came second to the Conservative Party in the remaining three parliamentary seats.

Penvollard: Economy and population

Penvollard exemplifies the changes that have occurred in Cornwall in the characteristics of its population and employment. From an economy based on mining and farming the town has lost local employment but gained commuters and people retiring to the area. The population of 1871 was 6,500 during the copper mining boom but then declined due to the loss of jobs in local industry. By the 1980s the area had the fastest growing population in the county. In the 1960s and 1970s housing development took place on the edge of the town. The population grew by nearly a fifth from the 1971 to the 1981 census with the proportion of elderly people declining to 22 per cent and with the largest group of incomers in the 25-34 age group, particularly young families.[1] Despite such growth, the population at the 1981 census was, at 6330, below the 1871 figure, but had overtaken it by the 1991 census. The growth of population without a corresponding growth in local employment was facilitated by improved road links. The improved access led to housing demand both from commuters and for retirement homes. The proportion of those in work who were self-employed was 26 per cent, a third of male workers. Outside the town a large proportion of the self-employed were farmers. Local employment was predominantly in the service sector, the main employers in Penvollard being the district council, social services and the local schools. There were problems in attracting new firms because of the relative remoteness of the area and a lack of many supporting industrial and commercial services. The town's industrial estates had a high proportion of service industries. Cornwall has the lowest percentage of employment in manufacturing in the south west at under 12 per cent (Plymouth Business School, 1995, p.1).

Penvollard was on the main rail link but there had been a decrease in all forms of public transport and transport was a problem for those without access to a car, particularly teenagers and the elderly. Teenagers complained of a lack of facilities for them. The town had a swimming pool, used by most children interviewed, and sports clubs including rugby, football and cricket. Play groups and mother and toddler groups met in the Anglican and Methodist church halls. There were uniformed organizations of Cubs, Scouts, Brownies, Guides, Girls' and Boys' brigades; youth clubs run by the Anglican and Methodist churches and a town band which played at carol services and concerts in churches. Although the provision of a venue for activities might not seem a particularly strong church connection, it did make the church and clergy known to many mothers with young children, and the contact was then reinforced through the primary schools which held services in church or chapel and had visits from clergy.

The divisions within the population of Cornwall were mirrored in the town. Newcomers tended to be owner occupiers living in the new housing estates on the edge of the town and to have been attracted by the physical features of the area and quality of life. Local people on low wages, especially the young, had problems finding housing with little council housing available. The local advice bureau reported that most problems were to do with unemployment, resulting debt, and housing.

Religion in Cornwall

Cornwall presents a rather different religious map to the rest of England due to the relative strength of Methodism and the under representation of both Catholics and the major non-Christian faiths. According to the English Church census of 1989, Church attendance in Cornwall was around the average of 10 per cent and child attendance was 17 per cent (Brierley, 1991b, p.24). However looking at attendance by denomination, over 44 per cent of adult attenders went to a Methodist church compared with around 11 per cent nationally. In all 54 per cent of adult attenders went to one of the Free churches, 28 per cent to an Anglican church and nearly 18 per cent to a Roman Catholic church. (Brierley, 1991, pp.6, 24)

The apparent strength of Methodism in Cornwall reflected a considerable decline from a high point reached in the late nineteenth century, before the population of Cornwall fell with the slump in mining and agriculture (Coleman 1991,p.151). The decline continues despite the population growth from the 1960s. According to the MARC Europe figures adult Methodist attendance in Cornwall dropped by 19 per cent from 1975 to 1989 and membership by a quarter in the same period

(Brierley, 1991, p.24). The figures for Anglican attendance showed a similar decline, 24 per cent since 1975. On the other hand the proportion of churchgoers who were Anglican had risen since the 1851 Religious Census figure of 19.3 per cent (Coleman, 1991, p.140). The diocese of Truro was not established until 1876 and the building of new churches and establishment of day schools since then has ensured a greater influence for Anglicanism in the county, while the strongholds of Methodism have continued to be eroded through economic change (Winter, 1991).

Migration into Cornwall affected all the denominations. The Roman Catholic Church increased its presence considerably from the late nineteenth century due to migration. The 1851 religious census figure for attendance at a Catholic church was less than half a per cent of overall attendance and seven places of worship were counted (Coleman, 1991, p.138). By 1989 the percentage of churchgoers who were Catholics had risen to 18 per cent but that figure was only just over half the average figure for England (Brierley, 1991b, p.6). The relative decline of Methodism in the twentieth century could be seen as part of an erosion of local identity. Those born in Cornwall and migrating out of the county were more likely to be Methodist than the considerable number of incomers, since Methodism was weaker in the south-east and west-midlands (Brierley, 1991a, map 3). Those who retained a nominal allegiance to a church tended to describe themselves as Church of England in Cornwall as in other parts of England. Thus the Rural Churches Project, which took parish samples from the Register of Electors as well as samples from the Anglican Church electoral rolls, found 68 per cent of the Cornish parish sample identified themselves as Church of England, nine per cent Methodist and two per cent Roman Catholic (Davies, Pack and Seymour, 1990, p.58). If nominal allegiance was proportional to attendance then the figures would have been 28, 44 and 18 per cent respectively.

Religion in Penvollard since 1851

In Penvollard the local religious organisations did not include any of the major non-Christian religions which would be found in many other parts of the country. The relative decline of Methodism and growth of Catholicism and Anglicanism can be shown by comparing the 1851 Religious Census figures with attendance in the late 1980s.

In 1851 the decline in mining had not yet taken place and the Poor Law Union of Penvollard had a population of 33,831 so, although the area experienced a rise in population in the 1960s and 1970s, the figures in the 1980s were not very different from those at the height of the mining boom (Mann, 1853, p.57). On the day the Religious Census was taken the total number of attenders at public worship was 8,081 in the morning, 4,986 in the afternoon and 6,860 in the evening (Mann, 1853, p.57). If all those figures were added together then almost 60 per cent of the total population of the Penvollard district attended worship. Attendance was below the average for Cornwall and almost the same as the average for England as a whole.

Using the method recommended by Pickering of `maximum-minimum' figures and looking at the highest single attendance figure for each denomination, 29.4 per cent of the total population attended public worship (Pickering, 1967,p.393). This overall figure was made up of 10.5 per cent Church of England and 17 per cent Methodist, comprising Wesleyan Methodist (11.2 per cent), Bible Christians (2.4 per cent) and Wesleyan Association (three per cent). Roman Catholic and Brethren each accounted for only 0.2 per cent of attendance (Mann, 1853, p.57). 1851 was a time of high Methodist membership although the peak for the Penvollard circuit was later, in 1863 for the Wesleyan Methodist and 1877 for the Bible Christians (Probert, 1971, p.55). At the time of the census the three Methodist groups had 63 chapels in the area, more than double the 31 Anglican churches.

In an attempt to make some sort of comparison with modern Penvollard, the current membership and attendance figures for the two Methodist chapels, the Anglican Church and other Christian groups were compared with the total adult population (table 5:1). The core of regular adult Church-goers attending mainstream Christian groups formed about eight per cent of the adult population in 1989. Some small groups were omitted, for example the Spiritualists and Jehovah's Witnesses, and other denominations were not represented in the town notably the Baptist and United Reformed Churches. Nearly 18 per cent of the adult population attended at the main festivals. If children, who tend to have a higher rate of attendance, were included in the figures the percentage who sometimes attended an ordinary Church service would be still higher. Through youth clubs and the uniformed organisations the various churches also made contact with young people who did not attend worship. The Anglican Church appeared to be much larger looking at membership but in terms of the size of the regular congregation it was roughly on a par with the Wesley Methodist, and, according to the chairman of the circuit, active Anglicans and Methodists were approximately equal in numbers. The Roman Catholic Church had increased its share of churchgoers since the 1851 Census due to migration.

Even though accurate comparisons over time are not possible, the week-by-week attendance has undoubtedly declined markedly from 1851 to 1989. However there did not seem to be a rejection of organised Christianity itself given the level of participation in church or chapel based activities, the school services in church or chapel and occasional attendance at public worship, as well as baptisms and weddings. The particular characteristics of the main denominations and their contact with children are considered next.

Table 5.1
Membership and adult attendance at places of worship, Penvollard, 1989

	Membership[a]	Main Service[b]	Festivals
Church of England	534	130	380
Methodist	202	180	380
Roman Catholic	56	50	60
Salvation Army	25	25	30
Association of God	24	20	20
Society of Friends	08	06	10
Total	849	421	880
% of Adult Population	17	08	18

Notes:
a. Definition of Membership:
    Church of England: electoral roll members
    Methodist: roll members of the two chapels in Penvollard.
    Roman Catholics: baptised and active (Penvollard only)
    Salvation Army: soldiers sworn in at 14 and over
    Assembly of God: baptised members
    Membership and attendance figures obtained from religious groups' own records and officials.
b. Main Service defined as the one with the highest attendance.
c. Adult population estimated as 5,031.

The Anglican Church

The Anglican Church in Penvollard had the largest electoral roll in Cornwall, 534 in 1988, down to 503 by 1996. Five much smaller village churches were included with Penvollard Church in a team ministry served by three clergymen and three lay readers. Although Anglo-Catholicism had been strong in Cornwall since the diocese was established, the churchmanship in the town's only Anglican church was evangelical and charismatic. There were regular 'Praise' services, services of healing and a charismatic group called 'Living Waters'. The Rector in 1992 had been at the church for thirty three years and had been chairman of the church school governors since its inception. The headmasters of the church school, county junior school and comprehensive school all attended the Anglican church, as did the head of religious education at the comprehensive school. There was therefore scope for developing close links between children, teachers and the church.

The Anglican church made it easy for parents to bring or send their young children to church. During the Sunday morning service there was an infant crèche, junior church for the under-tens divided into age groups and Pathfinders for ages 10-14. Older teenagers attended Cyfa on Sunday evenings and took part in the monthly 'Praise' service. The leader of the junior church had been a Baptist and the leader of Pathfinders was a Roman Catholic. The aim of the teaching was to lead children to a personal faith rather than to give Anglican teaching and so the leader of Pathfinders felt that being a Roman Catholic;

> doesn't make a difference. [We are] trying to communicate with them and get an understanding of the faith ... we don't teach commitment to the Church but to Christ. (Leader of Pathfinders at the Anglican church)

Teaching material from the Scripture Union, 'Pilot', was used with the children in Pathfinders rather than specifically Anglican material. The children did a variety of Bible based activities including poster making, games, quizzes and drama. About 30 children were on the register, most coming regularly to the weekly Club night and about twelve coming regularly on Sundays. The proportion of boys was lower on Sundays. Most of the children went, or had been, to the Church school, some coming as a result of the leader of Pathfinders visiting Year 6 in the Church school just before they left and inviting them to a disco. Children tended to come with friends and their parents did not necessarily attend church. Pathfinders did not attend full services in church other than the family services which were aimed particularly at young children. Both the Rector and the leader of Pathfinders said that the children enjoyed being in a group but were more reluctant to go into Church. The decision to be confirmed was becoming an adult decision rather than the culmination of 'Sunday school' teaching and so children were unlikely to be confirmed when they left Pathfinders at fourteen years old except for the minority who came from committed church families.[2] The majority of children, who came with friends rather than parents, did not begin to attend normal services once they had outgrown Pathfinders. Some would join Cyfa, which met on Sunday evenings, and was started so that children 'had somewhere to go' having left Pathfinders (Leader of Pathfinders). In 1989 twelve girls and two boys belonged to the group.

Through the play group held in the Church hall and the Church school and nursery, members of the team ministry had contact with a significant proportion of young children in the town who would not necessarily attend a normal Sunday service or junior church group. Because most contact was made with young children, mothers tended to be involved rather than fathers, and play group, nursery and primary school teachers were mainly female. Church groups for young people were also predominantly female and became more so going up the age range as girls continued to attend Pathfinders or Cyfa without their parents. Confirmation candidates were more likely to be girls and women and the Rector reported that this had been the case since he came to the parish over thirty years before. Figures for the whole diocese show that more girls/women were confirmed in higher numbers in most years throughout the century. From 1900 to 1965 the only years when more men than women were confirmed were 1915 and 1940, presumably due to the numbers of servicemen being stationed in Cornwall during the two world wars.[3] Men were of course involved in the Anglican church as leaders in youth groups, members of the team ministry and head teacher and deputy head of the Church school.

Methodist chapels

The Wesley Methodist in Penvollard had a membership of 179 in 1988, nearly three times as large as any other chapel on the circuit and 24 per cent of the total circuit membership. Membership had fallen slightly to 153 in 1996. In contrast, twenty of the chapels on the circuit had between one and twenty members. The Wesley Methodist, like the Anglican Church, had relatively large congregations and facilities for various groups to meet (table 5.1). The morning service was attended by around 200 people including about 20 children and the evening service by 40-60 people. Special services at Easter and Harvest might attract up to 400 people. Monthly communion services were being introduced by the new minister (1989), replacing quarterly ones, and there were to be some family communion services as part of the morning service when children could come up to be blessed, or, to take communion if they wished. Young people would not become members before their late 'teens. The membership class in 1989 had five young people in it, the youngest of whom was eighteen. Chapel members commented on the turnover of people moving into and out of the town and the need for young people to leave the area for higher education.

The Wesley Methodist still had contact with many children whose parents were not churchgoers. The majority of children attending the junior church came without a parent. In all, sixty one children were on the registers for junior church and thirty five were members of the youth club, 'Way In', which met twice a week and had a waiting list. Although run by church members in the church building, the youth club was open to all. Twenty five girls, aged five to fifteen, belonged to the Girls' Brigade and eleven boys, aged six to sixteen, to the Boys' Brigade. For older teenagers, aged 16 to 18, there was 'Focus' which met on Sunday evenings. For pre-school children there was a Mother and Toddler group and a Sunday morning crèche. The 'cradle roll', which recorded children under three years old, baptised at the chapel and living in the area, had seventeen children on it in 1988. The secretary delivered a card to children on their first three birthdays and at three years old they were invited to join the junior church. About half of the children on the roll had no other contact with the chapel, illustrating the existence of nominal membership more often associated with the Church of England.

Volunteers ran a coffee shop 'Manna', open daily and selling Christian books and magazines and Traidcraft products. Having a central position in the town the coffee shop was used by a wider group of people than would attend the church. Organisations for adults included a young adults group, a drama group 'S'truth' run by a nineteen year old member of the chapel and a singing group 'Oasis'. About twenty five older members belonged to the Wesleyan Guild which had weekly meetings in the winter. The various activities were overseen by the Family Committee.

Children attended the Junior Church from age three to about fifteen when they tended to drop out, although there was a group for older teenagers. The leader of the Junior Church saw his task as 'trying to bridge the gap between the congregation and the young ' and to 'reach out' through the youth club to those who had no other contact with the chapel. There were fourteen teachers in the Junior Church in September 1988. The leader was a farmer with young children who had been brought up as a Methodist and whose wife was a lay preacher. Children stayed in for the first part of the service and had a short children's address before they went out to the Junior Church. Material from the Scripture Union had been used for teaching and had what the leader described as 'an evangelical bias'. It was being replaced by more specifically Methodist material. Video recorders and overhead projectors, a library, attractively decorated rooms and modern teaching methods were used, and constantly updated, to try to match the provision in the children's day schools. World religions, which were not part of the Church of England school syllabus, were included in the Junior Church and justified to the congregation in an issue of the magazine 'Bridge Builder'. The teacher hoped that looking at other religions;

> will give children a firm foundation in the Christian faith as they move into the wider world beyond Penvollard and come into contact with these other faiths. (Bridge Builder August 1988)

The leader emphasised the ethos of the Junior Church rather than specific teaching;

> we try to make the atmosphere happy ... children forget the facts but they remember the atmosphere [and may] go back to their roots

voluntarily once they have grown-up ... it is not so much what you do as how you go about doing it. (Leader of Wesley Junior Church)

The glorious past? To a certain extent the Wesley Methodist Church still provided, in the late 1980s, a focal point for social activities as well as Sunday worship. However, comparison with the activities of previous generations provided abundant evidence of the decline of the Church as a central part of social life. The Church was built in 1841 and then rebuilt in 1846 after an arson attack. Since then membership numbers have fluctuated due to secession and expulsion as new Methodist groups formed or disbanded. For example, there were five separate circuits in the town in 1849. In 1856 the average attendance was about 500, according to a later estimate but in 1853 there were only 160 members due to the formation of the Wesleyan Reformers (Bolitho, 1967, pp. 23f). In 1860 the total number of members of all the Methodist groups in the area, including the Bible Christians, the Wesleyan Reformers, the Free Methodists, the Primitive Methodists was estimated to be over 2,000.

In 1890 when the new Sunday school building at the Wesley Methodist was opened, there were 360 scholars in 22 classes with separate rooms and 34 teachers.[4] Two young men's classes had 66 members in total and a young women's class had 35 members. Other activities included a Young Men's Institute; the Mutual Improvement Society which held classes in shorthand, mathematics and English; a reading room equipped with magazines and open fourteen hours daily; a gymnastic class; cycling; cricket and camping. The chapel thus provided a social centre for large numbers of people of all ages.

In 1901 a cutting from the Cornish Times about the Wesleyan Teachers' Convention held in the town revealed a total of 765 scholars and 162 teachers in the local circuit. The Wesley Methodist had 358 scholars and 37 teachers Classes were held morning and afternoon at the Wesley Methodist chapel but in 1910 a meeting of teachers reported a decrease in average attendance on Sunday afternoons which was thought to be due to the summer or to the 'increased spirit of wandering that had attacked many young people on Sunday afternoons' (Sunday School Council Minute Book, 14.10.1910). The Sunday school was not transferred to the morning until March 7th 1965 when it was renamed Youth Church (Bolitho, 1967, pp. 18f). The children then attended the beginning of the service as they did in the 1980s.

Numbers on the cradle roll earlier in the century did not differ greatly from the 1988 figure. From 1915 to 1933 there was a maximum of 28 children on the roll (1915) and as few as three (1929). The much larger attendance at Sunday school earlier in the century could be due to the large number of older children attending. For example, in 1907 there were 173 scholars of over fifteen years old registered but only 46 under seven years old. By the 1980s children left junior church at a younger age but there were 39 per cent of the 1907 figures in the 3-7 age group. In 1927 there were 22 children aged four and five on the registers compared with 10 children aged 3-5 in 1988. The peak age for children's involvement had gone down and the proportion of boys had decreased. Boys were the minority, as they were at the Anglican Church, rather than the majority as they had been in the past.[5]

The other chapel in Penvollard was built in 1838 for the Wesleyan Methodist Association which seceded from the Wesleyan circuit in 1837 (Bolitho, 1967, pp. 18f). In 1988 it had a membership of 23 which had risen to 32 by 1996 mainly due to older people moving from the Wesleyan church when the morning service changed to an earlier time. A local lay preacher who took services there reported that no one was under fifty years old once the children had gone out and the congregation consisted of 'old [Penvollard] people a stable congregation unlike the Wesley'. There was a small Sunday school with children sent because their grandparents had been, rather than going with their parents.

The Catholic church

The Catholic church served a large parish measuring twenty five miles across. The first church was built in 1832 and, according to the priest, the present enlarged church was built in 1863 to accommodate the influx of Irish people coming to work in the tin mines. There were 170 people who attended the church in 1989, about a third from Penvollard itself, very few of whom were born in Cornwall. [6] The congregation had been composed mainly of elderly people retiring to the area but, with the new housing and influx of commuters, more young families had joined in recent years. There were few teenagers since most of those moving in had only young children. There was no Catholic school in the town and only four in the whole county, but a 'bus service was started in 1988 to take children from Cornwall to the nearest Catholic primary and comprehensive schools. About 50 children living within thirty miles of these schools used the service in its first year.

In 1988 there were eight baptisms, six first communions, one wedding, one funeral and mass attendance of 160 (Plymouth Diocese Year Book, 1989, p.113). There were no specific organisations for children to belong to and children attended the normal services.[7] Active organisations attached to the Church were the Catholic Women's League and a Bridge club.

The Anglican Church

Interior of the Wesley Methodist Chapel, built 1846

Temperance rally in Penvollard, 1907

Building Kingdom Hall, 1989

The Salvation Army

The Salvation Army had a citadel in the town which celebrated its centenary in 1987. It was run by a married couple. There were 25 adult members and six junior soldiers in 1989, most of whom had not been brought up in the Salvation Army. A weekly 'Adventure club' for 5-15 year olds was attended by 20-25 children, about equal numbers of girls and boys. The religious aspect was described as 'low key' by the Captain, who did not wear uniform at the club. Sunday school on Sunday afternoons was attended by 10-15 children ages 5-14 and used Scripture Union teaching material. Other activities included weekly coffee mornings, over 60s and ladies meetings, which involved people who did not attend services, and a small band and 'Songsters' for uniformed members.

The Society of Friends

The Society of Friends, or Quakers, met twice a month in the public rooms in Penvollard. There were only eight members in the Penvollard area and only two from the town itself. There were no children's meetings. Remnants of a greater presence could be seen in the Penvollard area. There was a row of Quaker cottages still standing and a burial ground just outside the town which was closed because it was full. However, by the 1851 Religious census, the Quakers had two places of worship in the Penvollard district attended by only 0.14 per cent of the population, almost the same as the 0.16 per cent of Penvollard's adult population attending in 1989 (Mann, 1853, p.57).

Assembly of God

The Assembly of God, a Pentecostal Church, had been in Penvollard since the early 1980s. Two Sunday services were held, a morning communion service and an evening 'gospel' meeting. The congregation were mainly middle aged or retired, which the Pastor considered unusual for a Pentecostal Church. He was attempting to attract more young people through door to door evangelism and the distribution of information. The usual morning congregation was eleven or twelve and a few more in the evening. Some of these people came from outside the town. In all twenty four people had been baptised. There was a Sunday school in the morning which was attended by up to six children.

Jehovah's Witnesses

The other main religious group was the Jehovah's Witnesses. There was a Jehovah's Witness Kingdom Hall built in 1989 on a site on an industrial estate on the outskirts of the town to replace a smaller building the other side of town built in 1965. There were five services a week and around 80 baptised members, but many of these came from outside Penvollard since the nearest alternative meeting places were 20 miles away. Children would not usually be baptised until the age of eighteen. There were no separate groups for children or teenagers as the emphasis was on the family coming together and children being involved with their parents in preaching work. Attendance at meetings in Kingdom Hall and other members' houses and door to door evangelism filled a large part of available leisure time for Witnesses, but, Kingdom Hall did not provide a centre for activities for children in the town in the same way as the Wesley Methodist or Anglican church buildings.

Other religious groups and ecumenicalism

Also represented in Penvollard and meeting in the public hall were the Spiritualist Church and the Christian Scientists. There was a House Church, the New Life Church which was renamed 'The Vine Church' in 1992 after merging with an Evangelical Fellowship in another town. The congregation met at Penvollard Junior school on Sundays and held Bible studies and prayer meetings during the week. The largest group outside the main denominations came into existence in 1994 when a Methodist minister from a nearby town had to leave the church due to his opposition to the Methodist views on homosexuality and multifaith issues. In 1996 his congregation, numbering around 200, met in the Public Hall but had acquired a property outside Penvollard to convert into a centre for worship. Local religious groups met together on the Council of Churches, the local ministers' luncheon meetings and the Bible society, chaired by the Salvation Army Captain in 1989. United evening services were held and exchanges of pulpit included the Catholic priest, as well as Anglicans, Methodists and the Salvation Army.

The 'Established' Church?

The usual contrast made between the Anglican Church and other churches is that the Anglican Church has a responsibility for everyone in the parish whereas the rest are congregational churches. While this would be true of all the smaller denominations and sects in Penvollard, including the Catholic Church, there was not such a clear-cut distinction between the two largest churches, the Anglican and the Wesley Methodist. The Wesley Methodists had in a sense been the established church in Cornwall with attendance in the 1851 Religious Census which were larger than the Anglican church and with more places of worship (Coleman, 1991, p.143). Other Methodist groups on their own almost equalled the Church of

England attendance. In the late 1980s the numbers were more equal and there were similarities in organisation and worship in the evangelical Anglican church and the 'high' Wesleyan Methodist. The organisation of the Anglican churches in the area had become more like the Methodist circuit by the combining of parishes and the increased use of lay people. Anglican churches in the area no longer had their own Vicar but operated with a team of clergy and lay readers covering Penvollard and five smaller village churches.

Both churches had nominal members and occasional attenders as shown in the much increased numbers for festivals and parents bringing children to be baptised who did not otherwise attend. Both churches had the majority of children attending Sunday Junior Church without a parent and ran club nights which included children who never attended services. However the leader of the Anglican 'Pathfinders' was planning to restrict weekday club nights to those who came on Sundays whereas the Methodist junior church leader saw the youth club as a way to meet children who would not attend church. The Wesley Methodist still had larger numbers of children attending Junior Church and particularly drew from the indigenous Cornish who were a declining proportion of the town's population. Children were confirmed in the Anglican Church but usually only if their parents were regular churchgoers. The Methodist Church was having more regular communion services and planning to allow children to take communion, while the Anglican Church was moving towards adult confirmation paralleled by adult membership in the Methodist Church. To the outsider denominational differences were not obvious in the teaching. Both churches used Scripture Union material in the Junior Church groups but it was in the Methodist Church that the material was thought to be 'evangelical in bias' and 'getting away from the Methodist line' (Leader of Junior church). The Anglican Church emphasised commitment to Christ rather than to the Church and had leaders and teachers from various denominational backgrounds.

The Anglican and Methodist Churches still had a prominent role in the community life of Penvollard, particularly involving the elderly and young children. Contact was made informally through social activities, Church and Chapel services, concerts and for all primary age children through the local schools.

Penvollard schools

Penvollard had two schools for junior age children, one a Church of England aided school and one a county school. From these schools and a nearby village school, the sample of families was drawn (see appendix 1). The village school was included as an example of a church school which served the local community rather than providing an alternative to a county school. To look at the role of these schools in the children's religious and moral development this section draws on interviews with head teachers, class teachers, governors, school handbooks and curriculum materials. In chapter 4 church schools were said to be distinctive in terms of their ethos and staffing, their relationship to the community, admissions policy, religious education and assemblies. The two Penvollard schools and the village school are therefore discussed under these headings. At 11 years old children from church and county schools usually went to the town's comprehensive school. There are no aided or grant maintained secondary schools in Cornwall.

Penvollard Church school

Penvollard Church school was opened in 1979 and was the eighth new aided school to be built under the Diocesan development plan in which it was decided to build new aided schools in all centres of population throughout Cornwall. These schools were to exist alongside LEA schools thus giving parents 'an alternative choice of a Christian based education'. That phrase from the school handbook illustrated the emphasis on Christian rather than denominational education. The headmaster of the county junior school commented on this;

> Church of England schools [are] calling themselves Christian unofficially. (county junior school headmaster)

The school was on the edge of the town in an estate of owner occupied housing built at the same time and close to an estate of council housing. There were about 250 children on the roll and a nursery. The school had had the same headmaster from its opening and he had thus had a major role in determining the ethos' of the school through its organisation, the appointment of staff, religious education curriculum and assemblies. Penvollard Parish Church was within walking distance on the edge of the old part of town. The Team Rector was the Chairman of the school's governing body. The headmaster lived locally, was a lay reader and attended the parish Church. He had trained in a Church of England college and taken divinity as his main subject.

Ethos and staff The school's curriculum document emphasised the role of the school as a caring community helping children to grow up as individuals but within the context of belonging; first to the family and then to the school and local community, and also to the wider world beyond. The caring atmosphere was said in the handbook to 'stem from a genuine love for God and for our fellow man'. The head had taught in different types of school and saw the aims as fairly similar but;

> the basic difference is that we try to provide an ethos undergirded by the Christian faith. (Penvollard Church school headmaster)

He stressed the importance of Christian teachers to maintain the distinctiveness of church schools.

> There must be pressure for both good teachers and committed Christians or there is no point in having church schools. ... the pressures are very great to take teachers who are not Christians ... the Church are too lax in appointments ... trying to please too many people and pressures from county hall override the influence of the Church. Can become very good schools but lose their Christian identity. (Penvollard Church school headmaster)

All advertisements for teaching posts stated that 'applicants must be committed Christians' a more stringent requirement for classroom teachers than most church schools.[8] The team Rector, as Chairman of the Governors, agreed that one non-Christian teacher can 'wreck the atmosphere' and said he 'would not accept a good teacher who was non-Christian'.

The issue was one on which some other governors, teachers and parents disagreed with the headmaster and Chairman and felt that Christian commitment was desirable but second to teaching ability;

> Must start with how good a teacher they are ... Not to take an indifferent teacher because they are Christian and pass over a good teacher. (Vicar/governor Penvollard Church school)

Several mothers made a similar point referring to a particular teacher.

> [They] take committed Christian teachers who are not necessarily very good. ... [They put] Christian beliefs before teaching ability. (mothers with children at Penvollard Church school)

The headmaster said he had changed the job description when looking for a science teacher, in order to make an appointment. He had altered the academic criteria rather than compromise on the religious criteria. . The deputy headmaster felt that there should be room for different teachers, some not particularly active but not agnostic or 'against religion'. He would be sympathetic rather than stringent when choosing teachers. For him the Christian ethos was more to do with relationships;

A church school is a happy large family as all primary schools should be. [It is] Christian in itself to be that. (deputy headmaster of Penvollard Church school)

Relationships with the community   The headmaster emphasised the importance of encouraging links with the local Anglican Church, its clergy and organisations like Tiny Tots and Pathfinders. Parents were urged to join in the life of the Church and, ideally, staff would also be involved in the local Church. The children attended the Parish Church at least once a term and clergy came into school regularly to take assemblies.

The school documentation stated that the school should be involved with the life of the town. There were money raising activities, loaning of school facilities to local organisations and visits to a local old peoples' home as well as participation by local people in school assemblies. About fifty parents helped in the school each week working alongside the teacher. They heard children read, took weekly clubs and served coffee after the class assembly. The headmaster did not see their involvement as a particular characteristic of a church school.

Admissions policy   The school was oversubscribed and operated an admissions policy with brothers and sisters of existing pupils having first preference, followed by those recommended by the vicar or minister of the family's church and, if a further division was necessary, committed Christians first. The school served as a deanery school so children from Church families outside Penvollard were also admitted. Of the 37 children in the last year of primary education, seven lived up to six miles outside the town and nearer to village schools, which in some cases were aided schools. The Rector/chairman of the Governors, explained that brothers and sisters accounted for a large percentage of admissions at the time of interview and many came from families whose elder child had been admitted when the school first opened, not all of whom were committed Christians. The school was popular with middle class parents including those in the new owner occupied homes around the school but had fewer from the surrounding council estate. The best predictor of whether children aged 10-11 would be at the Church school or the county junior school was whether they lived in a council or a private house. Both the Rector and the headmaster were aware that some parents were more likely to apply than others;

the middle class are better at getting round to putting their children's names down [for the nursery unit] ... the school reflects church attendance. [It is] sad, parents could be drawn into the church through the school. (Penvollard Church school headmaster)

81

The nursery unit gave priority to 'council house parents' according to the headmaster, but not all the nursery children could be accommodated in the reception infant class. The Rector commented;

> We are not going to get some of the rougher children because it would not occur to their parents to apply. Some go to the nursery and might come in that way. (Rector/chairman of governors)

Since only 32 children out of the 50 in the nursery unit could be admitted to the school the criteria referred to above were important in the selection. The interviews with mothers of children in the school and at the county junior school showed that the middle class mothers were willing to find out the admissions policy and meet the criteria if they felt the school was the one to which their children should go. Working class mothers were more likely to rely on rumours, for example, 'your child has to be baptised to go there'. In fact baptism rates among those interviewed were broadly similar (72 per cent in the Church school and 64 per cent in the county junior school, including Methodist, Catholic and Anglican baptisms). The Diocesan Director of Education for the diocese particularly stated the need to ensure that 'less articulate parents understand the criteria'. However it was not so much that practising Christian families were being excluded as that 'more articulate' parents were prepared to meet the criteria, if only temporarily.

Four of the governors gave specific examples of the ways parents got their children into the school. For instance the Rector described a woman whose husband was in a professional job and who;

> moved heaven and earth to get her kids in. She did get them in in the end because she met the criteria then spent the whole time they were there complaining that there was too much religion. (Rector/chairman of governors)

Another governor mentioned a parent who had;

> brought the child religiously [to church] from the day they were born until they went to [the Church] school and had not been seen since. (Vicar/governor of Penvollard Church school)

Religious education The syllabus for religious education was prepared by the headmaster and based on the Bible. The school booklet stated that the basic aim;

> is to give children some understanding of what the Christian faith is about. This involves teaching from the Old and New Testaments,

82

especially the life and teaching of Jesus ... considering the lives of famous Christians, sharing in a daily assembly and encouraging links with various organisations of the Church.

Since the headmaster wrote the syllabus and took each class once a week for religious education his views could be taken as a reliable indication of what was actually taught to children. He described himself as 'a conservative, evangelical Christian' and saw his aim in religious education as being to, 'Teach as clearly and simply as possible the truths of the Bible' and to apply them to the children's lives and the world today.

The Diocesan working party report on church aided schools, in 1988, stated that confessional RE was now discredited and both Anglican teaching and world religions should be taught 'in the same open way and with the same aim' (Truro Diocese, 1988, p.11). In Penvollard church school world religions were not taught and the approach was confessional rather than the recommended 'phenomenological approach'. It is doubtful if many church or county schools would have taught RE in the way the Diocesan report laid down, not least because it would require up-to-date knowledge of a subject in which few teachers specialised. Furthermore, few schools would have children from non-Christian backgrounds to provide an impetus for change. Penvollard drew criticism from some parents not because the RE assumed children were Christian but because they felt it exceeded the normal amount and religion encroached on other more important matters including the selection of staff.

Assemblies An assembly was held every morning and lasted at least half an hour. A member of the Church of England team ministry took one assembly a week and each class took it in turns to take the Wednesday assembly. Parents and their younger children were invited to the class assemblies and about eighty attended each week and could have coffee afterwards.

The headmaster outlined the first aim of assemblies as learning to worship a living God through praise and prayer, and enjoying it. Secondly assemblies aimed to teach children about the main festivals of the Church's year and the truths of the Bible through video and film, visits from local Christians, drama and the active participation of the children. Finally assemblies were a time for drawing the school together as an identifiable unit and so giving children a sense of belonging. Events in the life of the school could be talked about including children and teams who had done well. Overall the headmaster felt it was important that children should enjoy assemblies and said he tried to avoid using them as an opportunity to moan at children. Children were encouraged to question what they heard and to stay behind to discuss the assembly with the headmaster or a visitor.

Religious education and assemblies provided the ethos within which teaching took place rather than simply timetabled slots in the school day.

The Diocesan staff had been concerned that in church schools the worship did not introduce children to Anglican liturgy and suggested that schools should celebrate the Eucharist so that worship is not 'relegated to the realms of childhood fantasies and celebrations' (Diocesan Director of Education). A Diocesan working party report recommended that 'baptism is complete initiation into the Christian church', so that children could receive communion without being confirmed (Truro Diocesan Board of Education, c.1995, para. 52).

The Church school was situated in a town where almost all the children were from homes which were at least nominally Christian. As a new school, able to select teachers and pupils, it was able to maintain a higher profile Christian ethos than would be the case in areas where there were no alternative schools or where the school had room to accept all who applied. The character of the school was particularly influenced by the headmaster as he was appointed when the school opened and was motivated by his own personal faith to make a school with a Christian identity.

Penvollard county junior school

The school admitted children from age 7 to 11 years, mainly from nearby infant school. Although children from throughout the town could apply for either the Church school or the county infant and junior schools the intake at the county schools came disproportionately from the town's council housing estates. The new headmaster, appointed in 1991, compiled statistics on the school's intake. The children typically lived in council or privately rented housing and were eligible for free school meals. A high proportion, compared with Penvollard and Cornwall as a whole, lived on income support, were in single parent households and in households without a car. Since the new Church school opened, numbers had fallen from a peak of 400 to around 190 and were expected to fall further. The Special Area class for remedial education was incorporated in the school and drew children from a wider area. The school had a male headteacher and seven other teachers, including the remedial teacher. The headmaster was appointed in 1969 when the school had had voluntary controlled status before the new Church school was built. He attended Penvollard parish church and sang in the choir.

Ethos and staff The importance of unity was emphasised by the headmaster in the school's Curriculum Statement and in interview. The William Tyndale school, notorious in 1976, was mentioned three times in the Statement.[9] The headmaster used the example of William Tyndale not to criticise any particular educational philosophy, but to argue that if the staff were united a school could be successful whatever philosophy was adopted. At William Tyndale there had been 'warring factions' among the staff, between advocates of varying degrees of 'progressivism' and 'traditionalism' in education, which ensured the school's downfall. The headmaster wanted his school to be one which teachers, governors and parents supported. He noted that it was parents' complaints and the withdrawal of children from William Tyndale school which prompted action by the Inner London Education Authority and School Inspectorate. It was important to establish 'a dialogue' between parents and teachers. The headmaster was generally opposed to the formalization of teaching and learning because

> Learning is exciting. Can you say something is learned for ever once it is ticked off on a chart? (Penvollard county junior school headmaster)

The most important thing which he felt children should be taught was 'adaptability' because no one knew what the future would be like. Whilst the Church school headmaster and governors stressed the Christian ethos and need for Christian teachers, the county junior school headmaster and governors stressed unity and the need for teachers who fitted in with existing staff. As a county school governor put it; 'One dissident can ruin a school'.

The headmaster said he organised the school around 'the Christian ethic', particularly stressing 'caring' not 'dogma'. All the county junior school governors who were interviewed were asked about the differences between their school and others in the area and they answered by referring to Penvollard Church school. All of them began by saying that there were no differences really, by which they meant educational differences, but then added that there might be more religious teaching, or involvement by the Church, in Penvollard Church school. None showed any awareness of the social differences which were paramount for the headmaster, perhaps because none had children at either school. The headmaster was conscious of the social differences between the two schools and the effect on his school.

> There is a nicer kind of child at [Penvollard Church school] ... the worst publicity for the Church. Parents choose [it] for the wrong reasons. It is sad that this has come about, because the Church provided education before the State. Now it is the needs of the greedy not the needy ... (county junior school headmaster)

Church schools had, he felt 'misfired ... they cause divisions'. Like the Church school headmaster, he realised that some types of parents were better able to fulfil the criteria for admission to the Church school;

There has been a sudden increase in baptisms, [the Rector] could tell you about that ... I wish they [the Church] would listen to the needs of the social services and the non-Christian. (county junior school headmaster)

Relationships with the community Caring was said in the curriculum statement to be 'not emotional sentiment but practical aid' and central to health education and religious education. The ways in which the school served the community were similar to the Church school. For example, harvest gifts were taken to the elderly, concerts held at Old People's Homes. Services for Harvest, Christmas and Easter were held at the Anglican parish church or the Methodist Church, to which parents were invited. Jehovah's Witness families attended the school and some described by the headmaster as 'actively non-church people', but no children from non-Christian faiths.

There were fewer parental helpers in the county junior school than in the Church school and parents were not invited in to assemblies. There was a Parent-Teacher Association which ran social events. The lesser involvement of parents may have been due to a combination of social class factors, the absence of infant age children and the pattern of contact being established by a headmaster appointed in 1969.

Admissions policy Unlike the Church school, the county junior school could take any child who wanted to come. The buildings could take up to 400 children, and had done so in the 1970s, but currently there were less than half that number. The headmaster was conscious of the contrast to the Church school; 'There is no waiting list ... if they are warm and breathing!'

The parents who were interviewed tended to have had older children who went to the school when it was the only one available, to have sent their children there because they were not churchgoers, or, because they had moved into the area and found that the Church school was full. The most obvious difference between the county school and Church school mothers that were interviewed was one of social class rather than churchgoing. Half the mothers from the county school and 41 per cent from the Church school never attended a church. Only one county school father had a professional or managerial job compared with 41 per cent of Church school fathers. The one professional family from the county school had moved to the area and found the Church school full. The difference in churchgoing was not sufficient to explain the class difference between the two groups of families. It seemed that middle class parents found out the criteria for admission to the Church school and then fulfilled them, confirming the points made by some critics of Church schools. Middle class parents would probably have been better able to fulfil *any* criteria, if they particularly wanted their child to attend one school rather than another.

86

Religious Education In the General Curriculum Statement in use when the children were first interviewed, religious education was put with 'Health'.

> RE has been linked to Health Education as in our schools we are not here to convert but to make morally aware our responsibility to our fellow men.

The teacher responsible for that section explained that; 'You cannot hammer home the first commandment with children who do not go to Church'. She had consulted members of staff who wanted the Third World included and a humanistic perspective, which emphasised the interdependence of men and nations. She summed up the aim of religious education as 'education for life'. The theme of caring was said, in the Curriculum Statement to 'swallow up the allotted RE time in the primary school'. Topics included 'Conservation', 'Sharing the World's Resources' and 'Charities who Care for People or Animals', topics which were said to give class teachers with or without Christian convictions 'plenty of scope'.

General curriculum aims were adopted from the D.E.S. document 'The school Curriculum' (1981). The fourth aim was;

> To instil respect for religious and moral values and tolerance of other races, religions and ways of life.

The governors who were interviewed thought that religious education should be part of the curriculum but all made a comment indicating limitations to it;

> They've got to be taught that side of it - don't put so much importance on it as [Church school] people do
> Must have RE in school, but I don't feel RE is important in school at all except as part of culture.
> As long as they are taught the basic details- don't need religion rammed into them all the time. (county junior school governors)

Assemblies There was a 'non-denominational' religious assembly each morning. The headmaster and the teacher responsible for religious education both said assembly was to start the day and get all the children together. The governors agreed with that view;

> Assemblies are important as a meeting not for worship ... the religious side. (county junior school governor)

None of the governors said assemblies were for worship. The values they might convey were 'a sense of belonging' rather than specifically Christian ones. The headmaster or deputy headmistress took four assemblies a week and class teachers organised the other assembly in turn. Parents were not invited to assemblies.

The county junior school had been affected by the opening of the Church school, with parents putting their children's names down before the school could acquire a reputation. They appeared to be attracted by the new buildings and the general reputation of church schools. Some parents living nearby were simply opting for their local school but parents from the council estate, which was also near the school, did not usually do so. The county junior school thus had a different social class profile and a disproportionate share of children with social problems and special needs, in addition to the Special Area class for remedial education. The population of Penvollard was still rising in the early 1990s with the construction of new houses and there were proposals for a new building for the county junior school. It remains to be seen whether a new building might attract some parents, especially if a nursery class was introduced, since these were two reasons given by parents for preferring Penvollard Church school.

The Village Church aided school

Whereas parents had specifically to choose Penvollard Church school for their children, most church schools in the county were small neighbourhood schools. The nearest aided church school to Penvollard was six miles south and served the surrounding rural area. Some children from the village travelled in to Penvollard Church school but there was no evidence of parents looking for a non - church school as an alternative, although the indigenous population were Methodist in background. At eleven children could go to Penvollard comprehensive school or to an 11-16 comprehensive about the same distance away in a seaside resort.

The village had a population of about 600 in a new owner occupied housing estate, older council housing, cottages and farms. There was an Anglican Church with an electoral roll of forty and an Anglo-Catholic tradition. Eleven of those on the roll attended from outside the parish. There was no Sunday school, because, according to the Rector, the Methodist chapel had always run one, and no choir. Four children served. Communicant figures from the Church's records for Christmas 1988 and Easter 1989 were ninety six and eighty two respectively. There was a small Methodist chapel, with a membership of eleven, built about 1840 for the Wesleyan Methodist Association and now part of the Penvollard circuit (Bolitho, 1967, p.19,). The Sunday school first started in 1856. Of the nine children who attended in 1988 seven were from farming families. A retired farmer who had begun teaching at Sunday school in the 1930s could 'never recall' a child attending from the new estate. His son was the organist and his daughter taught with him in Sunday school which two of his grandsons attended. The numbers in the Sunday school registers were twenty two in 1960 but only three in 1947 and eleven in 1949. However there had been two services a day and an afternoon Sunday school in the 1930s rather than the one morning service of the 1980s.

The school was situated near the Church, Rectory and village hall. The local Rector was chairman of the governors. There were eighty five children on the roll in 1986, in four classes covering the age range from rising fives to eleven. The male headteacher had been in post for eight years and taught the top class. He had trained at a Church of England training college, and, like the head of Penvollard church school, he was an Anglican lay reader. He did not attend the local church as he lived about twenty miles from the school.

Ethos and staff The headmaster emphasised Christian teaching as integral to the school and the religious life as advantageous;

> [This is] a village school and religion is part of the package. There are more advantages than disadvantages [of a religious life]. Society is very wound up at the moment, bad things are happening. The Christian background goes some way to ordering life. (village church school headmaster)

The curriculum was based on an 'environmental approach' using first hand knowledge and experiences which included experiences of Christian living through the school.

> We do all the things other schools do plus the Christian dimension which is critical. (village church school headmaster)

The headmaster stressed the importance of Christian attitudes in teachers. He equated Christian attitudes with humane attitudes and 'reasonableness'. He looked for teachers who were 'broadly Christian' and did not advertise specifically for practising Christian teachers. Both he and the village Rector thought they were only allowed to specify commitment when appointing a headteacher, but candidates were asked about their religion in interview.

> Most teachers have Christian or humane attitudes, that's what it means. I look for Christian attitudes, a reasonable person. (village church school headmaster)

The local Rector and chairman of the governors stressed the general ethos rather than specific Christian teaching and hoped that children would leave the school;

> ... with the impression that the Church has something to say to them, not in teaching the parables but in exercising care and concern for them which they would associate with me or with the Church. (village Rector/chairman of governors)

The Rector and the other governors who were interviewed were conscious that the school was the village school and it could not be assumed that parents were committed to Christianity.

> It is not fair on non-Christian people that their children should be brainwashed. (farmer's wife and governor with children at the school)

Another governor with grandchildren at the school felt that church schools might encourage differences between denominations which was undesirable. The deputy headmistress felt that there should not be separate schools for some groups in a multi-cultural society and not for others. Since she did not like the idea of Muslim schools she felt there should not be church schools either. Instead the parents should give religious teaching at home. She and the two lay governors who were interviewed stressed the moral values which a church school could impart. They thought that morality was based on Christian values but would be acceptable for all parents, as Christian was equated with care for individuals.

Relationship with the community The deputy headmistress had been at the school since 1956 (sic) and had seen the change from a mainly agricultural community to a more socially and economically mixed population, with many commuting to nearby towns to work. The school attended church once or twice a term for Saints' days, Harvest and at the end of each term. The Rector was frequently in school and took a weekly assembly and religious education classes. He had started a youth club which was attended by many children from the school. He regarded the link with the school as a valuable one because he got to know children whom he would not usually meet.

The village looked like a traditional community to an outsider with church, school, village hall, pub and shops. However the people living there now had a greater ability to choose how far their lives would be centred on the village. In the past women could only work locally in farm and domestic work whereas now most families had cars and there was no longer what the deputy head described as 'a forced community'. The children interviewed all travelled outside the village for leisure activities; such as uniformed organisations and sport. In the top year, half the children lived about three miles away from the school in other villages. Denominational differences between incomers and locals were apparent. All the children attending the Methodist chapel's Sunday school came from local families, almost all farming families, whereas the Anglican church provided a 'high church' alternative to Penvollard Church and attracted people from outside the parish.

Parents did not come into the classroom, although one helped with cookery and there was a Parent Teachers' Association. Parents did not attend assemblies but did attend the church services held for the school. Both the headteacher and deputy distinguished between the locals and the people who had moved into the area. The latter were seen as more 'pushy' and 'critical' of teachers. Both teachers were wary of involving parents because of their possible criticisms of the school and their lack of professionalism.

Admissions policy The school had been able to take all those who wanted to come and the parents interviewed had sent their children to the school because it was the local one. One mother had hoped discipline would be better in a church school, and so had chosen the school rather than a county school about the same distance away.

Religious Education The headmaster emphasised the development of caring attitudes through the various topics and themes in which religious education was taught. There was no set syllabus. His class had been doing a topic for harvest. The topic integrated all subjects through looking at food, food production and the Rector 'comes in and does the religious aspect'. The Rector took each class once a week, spending about half an hour with the top class and less with younger ones. He went through the church's year, the history of the Church and church worship linked with the life of Jesus. He saw his role as an 'animator' who tried to animate children in the Christian way and give them a start in the religious life. Confirmation classes were announced in school. Although he was a young man recently trained, he had not been prepared for teaching since neither church schools nor children were mentioned in his training. The children and mothers who were interviewed were enthusiastic about 'Father Mark'. The Church of England based teaching depended on a clergyman or woman willing and able to come in regularly. 'Father Mark' later left and was replaced by a non-stipendary clergyman who did not live in the village rectory.

Assemblies The main purpose of assemblies was to worship God, according to the information sheet given to parents. The curriculum

91

statement described assembly as a service with hymns, readings from the Bible and other appropriate books, prayers and drama. The headmaster said that assemblies also had a teaching element since Christian living was taught throughout the year through a thematic approach. The headmaster took two whole school assemblies each week and the Rector took one. The BBC broadcast was used by the older children one day and individual classes had prayers the other day. The Rector also said that assemblies were to worship and pray to God. The other governors agreed with the county school governors in seeing them as times for the children to meet together.

The Diocesan Director of Education, who had been appointed from outside the county, was more cautious about stating the aims of assemblies in a church school.

> I am open minded on this. If there is a consensus in the community that children should worship then OK., and I am told that there still is that consensus in Cornwall, there is not in other areas. It cannot be worship when children from other faiths are in the school. (Diocesan Director of Education)

The village church school gave children a specifically Anglican education because of the link with the local church and Rector. The religious education was centred on the church whereas in Penvollard church school it was centred on the Bible. In Penvollard church school the emphasis on Christian teaching came from the headmaster who took each class for religious education. In the village school it came from the Rector. The non-stipendary minister who replaced him did not live in the village and was not able to maintain the same contact with the school.

All three schools had male headteachers who were practising Anglicans and two of whom were lay readers. The chairmen of the governors of both church schools were clergymen and the county junior school chairman was a church warden. It would be difficult to predict the ethos of a school or the nature of religious education and assemblies simply by knowing that it had aided status and was either a village or town school. The Diocesan Education Advisor felt that there should be a variety within the aided sector with town schools having a stronger identity than village schools. What actually went on in the church schools depended on the headteachers and their chair of governors and was therefore liable to change as the personnel changed. Religious education was particularly idiosyncratic. Roman Catholic schools appeared to have a more stable identity as 'catholic schools for catholic children'.[10] Whether they were catholic or not, parents knew what to expect from a catholic school. The village church school also met parental expectations of what an Anglican school would be like but Penvollard Church school did not.

Conclusion

The mothers and children whose religious beliefs, values and practice will be discussed in the next chapter, were living in a small community in which, despite an influx of population, the churches and Christianity continued to have a role in education and in general social life. The established churches, Methodist and Anglican, continued to provide services for the children of the uncommitted which were generally appreciated by parents. The number of religious groups available to attend was increasing rather than declining but the newer groups did not impinge on the lives of the non-members unless they attempted to evangelise in which case the most common reaction from the mothers was hostility. The tolerance towards religion depended on religious people keeping their views to themselves or expressing them in such socially acceptable ways as organising a youth club or luncheon club for the elderly. Having described the community of Penvollard the next chapter discusses the religious attitudes, beliefs and practice of some of the children and their mothers who live there.

Notes

1. The figures quoted in this section are taken from the district council's local plan for Penvollard, published in 1985.
2. In 1991, 13 adults and 13 children were confirmed and there were three recommitments.
3. Statistics obtained from the Central Boards of Finance of the Church of England, Church House, Great Smith Street, London SW1P 3NZ.
4. Statistics and other information in this section is taken from material in the Wesley Methodist church archives.
5. For example boys were in a majority according to the Sunday School Registers in 1890, 1927 and 1938.
6. Information in this section came from the priest who was also secretary of the Diocesan Schools Commission.
7. As has been the usual practice in catholic churches e.g. Brierley (1991a) does not record Sunday school figures for catholic churches, table 41. p.102.
8. For example, there were 24 advertisements for classroom teachers in Church of England aided schools in the Church Times, 15.6.90, and none required a practising Christian or Anglican. It is more usual to have such a requirement for head teachers.
9. Events at William Tyndale school in Islington led to a public inquiry, the report of which was published in 1976 (Auld, R., (1976), *William Tyndale Junior and Infant Schools Public Inquiry*, ILEA:

London). In the press the affair was presented as one of `left-wing' teachers versus parents anxious to preserve their children's standard of education. An account of the controversy is presented in Gretton, J. and Jackson, M. (1976), *William Tyndale: Collapse of a School or a System?* Allen and Unwin: London

10. See postscript pp.120 .

6 Religion in the home

We never talk about religion, it doesn't come up
I feel I am a Christian
Christianity is everything to me - my life (Penvollard mothers)

The purpose of the interviews with mothers and children was to gain an overall picture of their religiosity, both in terms of conventional organised religion (beliefs, attitudes and practice) and, more broadly, their core values. The structured questions provided a framework, at the first two interviews, for gathering information and monitoring changes. The comments made and experiences related provided some insight into the mothers' and children's understandings and, with the background knowledge of Penvollard, a way of explaining the patterns of responses. The questionnaire and details of the methodology are contained in appendix 1. The findings are presented in five sections covering;

1   Religious life history
2.   Religious beliefs and children's ideas about God and the church.
3   Mothers' views on religion and being religious
4   Attitudes to religion in school
5   Differences between Penvollard schools

Religious life history

In the religious life history of mothers and children generation, gender and social class are seen to influence church attendance. The decline in church attendance through childhood is monitored alongside the increase in churchgoing among mothers when their children were young. Among the children churchgoing becomes increasingly a girl dominated activity. The table and figures in this section (table 6.1, figures 6.1 - 6.4) detail the

95

church attendance of mothers and children with material taken from their religious life histories.

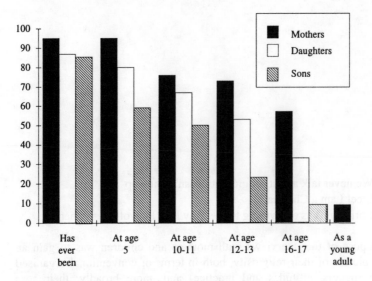

Figure 6.1 Church attendance of mothers and children
* Data for children only available to age of 17

Table 6.1
Church attendance of mother by social class*

Church Going	Child age 10 - 11		Child age 12 - 13	
	% middle class	% working class	% middle class	% working class
Regularly	22	16	17	16
Sometimes	56	26	44	16
Never	22	58	39	68
Total	100	100	100	100
(N)	(18)	(19)	(18)	(19)

*Classed by occupation/last occupation of main or sole earner at first interview. Only three women worked full time, two had same class as husbands and third was divorced and classed by her own occupation.

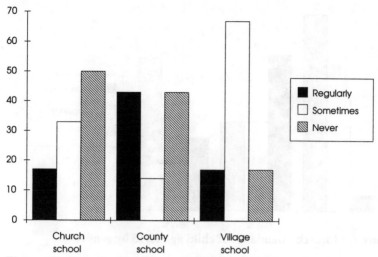

Figure 6.2 Church attendance of child age 10/11 by school

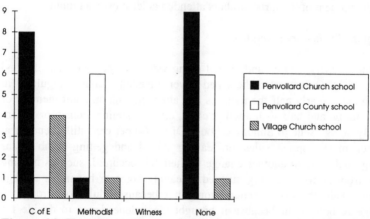

Figure 6.3 Church attendance of child age 10/11 by denomination and school

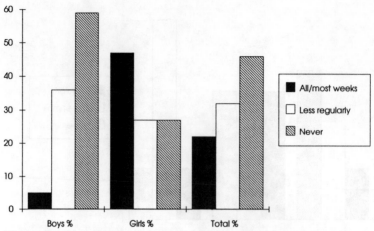

Figure 6.4 Church attendance of child age 12/13 by gender

Note: The attendance of the mothers could not account for the difference between boys' and girls' own attendance. 18 per cent of the boys' mothers and 20 per cent of the girls' mothers attended at least once a month.

Religious life history of mothers

For the mothers, church and chapel going was a normal part of childhood (figure 6.1). Only two mothers had never attended a church regularly in childhood. Nearly half the mothers had attended with an adult member of their family, and half with another child, either a sibling, cousin or friend, usually being 'sent' to Sunday school. Of the 60 per cent still attending at thirteen most stopped either on leaving school and getting a job or, as young adults, when another change in their life occurred, such as moving away from home or getting married. Leaving home or becoming a wage earner meant the end of churchgoing not because adulthood brought a change in belief, but because it brought the independence to decide for themselves, and often, a move way from the particular church they had attended. Having been influenced by their families to attend they were more likely to be influenced by friends and husbands not to attend as young adults. Whereas some mothers referred to their husbands as 'non-believers' or 'atheists' none referred to themselves in those terms. A gender pattern found in other studies.

Most of the mothers had changed denomination during the time they attended a church. In all cases this was because they started off in the denomination to which their parents or grandparents belonged and then made their own choice later on, either in adolescence or adulthood. The largest group (52 per cent of those who had changed) had been Methodist and then gone to an Anglican Church, attracted for a variety of reasons. This was, perhaps, a particularly Cornish version of a general tendency to change denomination. Similar findings by Toon and Towler in their research in Leeds, led them to argue that denominations are increasingly irrelevant (Toon and Towler, 1983). In adolescence the change was always made with someone of their own age, so the attraction might have been partly to assert their independence. As one woman recalled;

> I was brought up Methodist, Father was a strong Methodist and made me go when I was young. Then me and my brother changed to the Church of England. There is something more positive about the Church of England. I stopped going when I was married, my husband is not a great believer, he is not baptised but I pushed for the boys to be baptised. I go to the Church of England occasionally, parades [older son in the Airforce Cadets] and festivals.

Those who changed denomination as adults had all had a period of non-attendance before going to another church. Most had practical reasons for the change, such as wanting to have a child baptised and so 'trying the C of E ', wanting to get a child into the local Church school or finding a church nearby with a good Sunday school. A husband said that his wife had gone regularly 'to the church and got involved to get the kids into the Church school', which explained why she had stopped going once the youngest son was four. Another woman had been to a healing service at the Spiritualist Church which, she felt, had cured her back problem. By the second interview she had become a 'medium and a healer' herself and attended meetings with her new husband-to-be. She gave a more spiritual interpretation of her initial contact with the Spiritualists, saying 'people who go there are people with problems, searching for something'.

Two women described conversion experiences which led them to renewed religious practice, as a Jehovah's Witness and in the Anglican Church respectively. One had left the Church of England Sunday school at fifteen and became a Jehovah's Witness as an adult after an initial doorstep meeting. She and her ex-husband were members for five years before being 'disfellowshipped' for smoking and drinking. She looks back on her time as a member with nostalgia;

> I know there is a God and a right religion, I have just slipped by the way. The Witnesses keep away from the world ... it's a better life than this one. If I could stop smoking and heavy drinking I could join again. I still think it was the best time of my life ... I have been

back about four times, the others are not allowed to talk to me, I just go and sit and listen.

The other woman who had a 'spiritual experience' had been brought up as a Roman Catholic, but found the Church 'very severe' in not allowing her a church wedding for her second marriage. She moved away from London with her new husband, who had been brought up in the Church of England, and still felt guilty that she had ceased to attend church;

> Then we went to the Vatican when on holiday in Rome and there was an open audience with the Pope. We were in the queue and they let us in. I was in tears. He has charisma ... when he came in and stood on the dais goodness flowed from him ... he was radiant. Even Paul [her husband] felt it. I came back and felt I should go to church ... but went to [Penvollard Church of England] rather than the Catholic Church. I felt part of the community there, I knew a lot of people there from school.

Several working mothers mentioned lack of time as one reason for their occasional churchgoing becoming even less frequent or ceasing altogether. However the group most likely to attend church were those mothers with non-manual jobs. Those who never attended were most likely to be in manual jobs.

Past and present religious practice of children

When comparing mothers' churchgoing with their children it was apparent that the children were ceasing to attend at a much earlier age (figure 6:1). Nearly a fifth of children attended only in the pre-school years going to the 'tiny tots' services, crèches and family services which have evolved since their mothers were children. Both the main churches in Penvollard catered for very young children and the Sunday school registers kept by the Methodist chapel show that the greatest decline in numbers has been among older children (p. 74).

As well as the influence of generation on churchgoing there was also an influence of gender. When sons and daughters are looked at separately the daughters are much closer to their mothers' generation. Boys were particularly likely to 'drop out' before school age, having been taken by their mothers but not wanting to continue, and between leaving primary school and the second year of the comprehensive school. Twice as many boys stopped going to church or Sunday school between the two interviews as did girls (27 per cent: 13 per cent). Most of the girls still attending at 12/13 did so without their mothers, going with a friend, a sister or alone. The explanation for this is that the girls were attending Sunday school or

Pathfinders but all the boys had left these groups by the age of 12/13 and it would be unusual in any of the churches for a 12/13 year old to attend the ordinary service without a parent other than as part of an organised group; i.e. in Sunday school, as a server or in a choir. The findings parallel those in Francis's study of teenage churchgoing (Francis, 1984b).

Thus boys were less likely to attend a church and particularly unlikely to attend regularly (figure 6:4). Regular attenders were 88 per cent girls. Three quarters of the boys did not enjoy going, according to their mothers, whereas three quarters of the girls did. Mothers were much more likely to encourage their sons than their daughters to go to church, presumably because the girls were attending willingly and often without their mothers, whereas the boys were going less regularly with their mothers. Confirmation was not expected of teenagers. All the mothers felt this was to be left to the individual child preferably when they were older. By age thirteen the two girls and one boy who were the most regular attenders at the Anglican Church Pathfinders group had been confirmed and no more were confirmed by 16/17. If the Methodist Church had had confirmation at the same age then some of the girls who attended Sunday school regularly would probably have been confirmed before churchgoing declined further in the later teens.

The girls who attended the Methodist chapel junior church and whose parents never attended would be unlikely to become members. According to the youth leaders more than half the children come without their parents but most tend to drop out at around the age of fifteen. It seems unlikely that the girls who had never attended an ordinary service in its entirety would become part of the adult church. Two girls were still occasional attenders at the Methodist Church by age 16/17 but they went to 'Focus', a Sunday evening group for older teenagers, rather than to an ordinary service. A study in Scotland found Sunday schools to have a small positive influence on later church going but indicated the need for churches to give attention to those outgrowing these groups (Francis, Gibson and Lankshear, 1991).

Looking at the children attending the three schools the striking differences were in the percentages of *regular* attenders, much higher in Penvollard county school because of the girls attending the Methodist Sunday school, and the higher number of *occasional* attenders in Penvollard Church of England school, all of whom attended Anglican churches (figure 6.2). That the difference in the pattern of attendance was due to the difference in denominational allegiance can be seen in table 6:5. The families with children at the county school were usually born locally, Methodist in background and working class whereas those with children at Penvollard Church school were usually from outside Cornwall, middle class and attending an Anglican Church occasionally although they might have been brought up in other denominations.

Case studies of the two children still attending regularly at age 16/17 are included in appendix 1.

Religious beliefs and children's ideas about God and the church

Mothers' religious beliefs

When looking at the religious practice of the mothers, only one mother referred to her disbelief as a reason for ceasing to go to church saying 'It was the religious side I couldn't cope with ... I don't go now because I don't believe in it'. The other mothers referred to social rather than religious changes in their lives. The statement 'There are some mysteries in life that science will never explain' (table 6.2) was intended to discover how many of the mothers and children saw everything as ultimately explainable through the progress of human scientific knowledge and how many would leave room for the supernatural, for other powers or for a god or gods. As the table shows almost all the mothers agreed and all had an opinion, whereas a group of children were uncertain but none of the girls disagreed and only one of the boys.

The second statement was more specific; 'there is a benevolent power behind the universe' (table 6:3); and was interpreted by most mothers as a statement about belief in one God, although some interpreted it in a more general way and said 'there is something there' or 'there must be something there'. Others said they believed in God or a power but were 'not sure if he is benevolent'. All who disagreed were non-Churchgoers but all except one had agreed with the first statement (table 6:2). Several mothers mentioned recent disasters, either personal or national, as a reason for either disagreeing or agreeing with the existence of a benevolent power. So one mother said she now disagreed with the statement, 'not with all those disasters' whereas another saw disasters as evidence of 'forces we don't understand'. A mother who agreed with the statement at the first interview was now unsure because of several deaths that had occurred in her family;

> Sometimes that makes me think. When things happen to you, you think it wouldn't have happened [if there was a God].

Whether or not they regarded themselves as Christians all the mothers had at least one Bible in the house, but most never read it. Most occasional readers were using it as a reference book for their children's' homework, especially at secondary school. The pattern was similar in both Penvollard schools and between mothers of boys and of girls.

Table 6.2
'There are some mysteries in life that science will never explain': attitudes of mothers and children

	Mothers 1st %	Mothers 2nd %	Daughters %	Sons %
Agree	92	97	80	76
No particular opinion	00	00	20	14
Disagree	08	03	00	10
(N)	(37)	(37)	(15)	(21)

Note: By the second interview one boy was no longer living with his mother and was not interviewed, his mother gave information on his churchgoing, schooling etc. In attitude questions, therefore, only 21 sons are included.

Table 6.3
'There is a benevolent power behind the universe': attitudes of mothers and children

	Mothers 1st %	Mothers 2nd %	Daughters %	Sons %
Agree	73	70	53	43
No particular opinion	22	16	27	33
Disagree	05	14	20	24
(N)	(37)	(37)	(15)	(21)

Children's religious beliefs

The children interviewed for the second time at age 12-13, were less likely than their mothers to agree with the statement, 'there is a benevolent or good power behind the universe'. The word good was added when the statement was read to children and to any mothers who seemed puzzled by the word benevolent. Since the percentage of mothers agreeing was, at 70 per cent, similar to large scale studies the much lower figure, 49 per cent, for both girls and boys may be significant. Another third of the children were unsure in both Penvollard schools.

Ideas about God Children were asked if they ever thought about what God might be like. Out of thirty six children three were definite that they did not believe. One offered an explanation for other peoples' beliefs;

> People could make things up and carry it on. It's a bit like ghosts I
> don't think there are ghosts either. It's just peoples' imaginations
> and it helps people to believe there is a God.

Four children had 'not thought about it' and another three thought there is a
God 'probably' but they did not think about it further. Three children only
thought about things like that in religious education lessons or homework.
Seven children had thought about God and had some doubts because 'we
don't really know', 'you can't prove it' or 'for very scientific reasons'. One
simply said he thought about deep things but did not know. Two boys
mentioned the suffering that God allows to go on. One boy added 'life's a
bit too short ... get on with it and have the best you can'.

Of those with specific ideas about God, ten mentioned a human or
superhuman image and six a spiritual image. The conventional picture of
an old man with a long beard up in the sky was described; 'sitting in an
armchair in a cloud', 'like Father Christmas only not in red and white'.
Several felt they should have grown out of this image, and recognised it as
the children's' Bible story sort of picture but did not offer any other image
with which to replace it. Three children saw God as an ordinary human
being , 'a normal man, nothing too strong about him'.

In the spiritual images God may be up in the sky but not in human form.
One child saw him as 'sort of behind the sun ... in the rays of the sun' and
another girl identified him with a star that she could sometimes see from
her bedroom.

> When I go to bed, my bed and looking out of the window is my little
> Church ... I am quite fascinated by the stars and I think he lives up
> there sometimes. There is one star that connects with him. I don't
> always see it but it is there.

Why do you think people go to Church? Six boys had not thought about it
or did not know but the rest of the children gave an answer. The largest
group thought people go to learn more 'about it' or 'about God', an emphasis
that might be expected from an age group used to learning in assemblies
and Sunday school. Another group stressed the strong belief of those who
go to Church. 'Most of them are committed Christians, like those at Living
Waters (a charismatic group). They like to do it'. 'It is part of their life,
they believe in it'. An equal number talked about an aspect of worship in
Church; people go to pray or sing, 'to praise the Lord', to 'listen to God' and
'to thank God'. A fifth of the children stressed the benefit to the individual
of going to Church; either socially or in the sense of relieving their worries
and removing guilt. People 'go to meet other people and make friends with
other people and learn things and relax and pray and relieve their minds'
said one boy, while his twin brother, interviewed separately, put it more

succinctly, 'people like to get together and nitter natter'. Only 15 per cent of the children thought the Vicar did not have an important job, in one case because he did not earn much money. Asked what the Vicar/Minister does children answered either in terms of his leadership, teaching and helping his congregation or saw his role as teaching people generally about Christianity. Children seemed to display more tolerance of churchgoers than their mothers, none made any critical comments but rather felt that the Vicar should be there to meet their needs.

> He takes the service and helps them. Pretty important because if they didn't have a Vicar they wouldn't know what to do when they went to Church. He mainly reads prayers and leads things. I suppose [his importance] depends on what you believe and how religious you are. Important to the religious, not so important to those who are not religious.

While the mothers emphasised that children should be able to make up their own minds about religion, in contrast to their own experience of being made to go to a church, the children took free choice over religious matters for granted. At the same time about a third of the children commented on the need to know about religion before making up your mind about it;

> If people are going to make up their own minds about whether they believe in God or not, they have got to have someone to tell them about God first. If they didn't have a Vicar lots of people wouldn't know about it.

Mothers' views on religion and being religious

Aspects of religion rated as important

Mothers were asked how important or unimportant they thought different aspects of religion to be. The most important aspects of religion according to the mothers, were the moral and social dimensions, how you live and help others. The rank order is given below and is taken from the second interview with mothers when the children were 12/13 years old.

1. Leading a good life
   Giving to others

2. Believing in God
   Personal prayer

3   Going to a place of worship

4   Being an active missionary in your community

The aspect of religion which provoked most comment and aroused strong feelings among the mothers, whether churchgoers or not, was that of missionary work in the community. Those who did rate it as 'important' specifically excluded 'knocking on doors', except for the Jehovah's Witness and ex-Witness mothers and the 'born again Christian' who referred to the terrace of houses where she lived as 'conversion row'. Some interpreted missionary work as 'helping out when you can' and applied it to their own activities, for example one mother who used her gifts of healing and another who counselled but without mentioning her Christian faith. Others who said missionary work was 'not important' went on to give more positive examples of community work, such as helping with Guides, being a good friend, passing on God's love by example rather than badgering people to believe what you believe. The public nature of active mission work was resented as a type of 'showing off', in the same way as going to church 'to be seen'. As one mother put it 'my husband is better for doing things on the quiet than the Jehovah's Witnesses knocking on doors'.

Mothers who tended to see religion as personal and private resented people 'trying to indoctrinate others with beliefs' when these should be a matter for each individual. They echoed the views of teenagers and teachers referred to in chapter 2. It was also assumed that someone doing missionary work would be trying to make others believe and go to a church, both aspects of religion that were seen as less significant than the moral and social aspects. As one women said, leading a good life 'comes before going to church. You can do a bit of good for someone rather than sitting in church and then criticising when you get outside'. The important thing was to show people by example, by leading a good life and then one would not 'need to go out and knock on doors'. 'Giving and helping others is important not going out and saying you should go to church every week'. Similar comments were made even by the practising Christian mothers. As a district nurse said ;

> I am not a door knocker, but I feel fortunate that my profession allows me to show that I am a Christian. I wear an open-necked shirt in my uniform and my cross is always visible ... leaves it up to people if they want to say anything. People have asked if I am a Christian and it has led to talking about it.

One mother summed up the resentment felt by others by saying 'the word missionary puts my back up'.

The largest group of mothers did say that they were 'fairly religious' or 'not unchristian'. The mothers did not see a necessary equation of Christianity and morality but they were aware that other people did so and they still felt that to say you are 'not religious' might be thought to imply that you are not moral. Thus they either replied that they were 'very' or 'fairly religious' or, if they said they were 'not religious', made it clear that they still had beliefs and moral values. Those who had a specific criticism to make of religious people, which for these mothers meant Christians, all made comments about people who put religious practice before concern for others. One criticised the teachers at her son's church school as the 'God squad', and another was critical of the Anglican Church that ignores important social issues. Another felt religious people neglected the sort of old and lonely people she met as a homecare attendant,

> A lot have been very religious all their life but once they are house bound the church forgets them. They would like someone to come and read a passage from the Bible to them. [It] would be more Christian than going to church and mixing with high society as they see it.

Both those who said they were 'fairly religious' and those who said they were 'religious', associated 'being religious' with undesirable characteristics The 'image' of a religious person was not very good even among those who might be seen as 'religious' because they were active in a church. As one 'born again' Christian put it, 'when people talk about being 'religious' I don't think of myself as that'. As in other studies the trait most often associated with being religious was hypocrisy (Hoggart, 1957, Ahern and Davie, 1987)). Not only was churchgoing less important than 'giving and helping' as indicated in the last section, but there was an assumption that those who attended church did not also act morally, as shown in the following comments from three different mothers.

> I try to be kind and good but I don't go to church every Sunday if you call that being religious. If you ask 'Are you a Christian?', if it means showing it that way [churchgoing], then no. If it means loving one another and showing it in everyday life then yes.
> I would say I am a Christian, doesn't mean you have to go to church. You can go to church three times on Sunday but not be a terribly good Christian. Christianity is about the Ten Commandments and a code of life.
> People go to church to be seen. You might be in church on Sunday and ... [husband suggested 'murder your granny?'] beat the children!

Mothers' would juxtapose an 'over the top' example of being religious with their own view, meaning that they would consider themselves religious but not in an extreme way. Examples of 'over the top' religiosity included 'singing hymns in their sleep', going to church three times on Sunday, believing all the nitty gritty, being one of those holy Joes always at church', reading the Bible together every night, being 'in and out of church' or 'very fervent'. The way in which they were religious themselves was, for around a third of mothers, helping and caring for others, something seen as neglected by churchgoers, and teaching children these values. Another third of mothers stressed their beliefs which they expressed privately rather than in public, 'I don't spout religion or ram it down anyone's throats. It is very personal to me'. Religion should belong to this private 'spiritual side' but was seen as usually more ostentatious. As one mother said 'no, I am not religious, I have my own private beliefs and keep them to myself'.

The mothers were therefore critical of the churchgoing missionary image of religion, which few of them would fit, because most saw themselves as at least 'fairly religious'. The mothers' views are a microcosm of the national picture presented in chapter 2; they dislike the public aspects of religion while not rejecting specific beliefs or occasional attendance.

Religion is something which children have to make up their own minds about

When their children were age ten or eleven the mothers in both town schools were more likely to 'agree strongly' with the statement than with any other. This was particularly striking in the county school where 57 per cent 'agreed strongly' compared with only 14 per cent agreeing or disagreeing strongly with any other statement. The Church school mothers were more likely to qualify their agreement by saying that children needed guidance when 'young' or 'very young'. By the second interview when children were twelve or thirteen years old over 80 per cent of mothers in both town schools simply agreed with the statement and fewer qualified it.

The same four mothers disagreed with the statement at both interviews two years apart and their case studies appear in appendix 1. All said religion was 'very important' to them and all of them saw their role as guiding children to make a later decision for themselves. Children have to be taught first before they can make a decision, you have 'to put something into them at this age' as the Witness mother said, then 'they will make a decision when they feel ready, around their early teens'. The two children still attending every week at age 16/17 had mothers with those opinions. They were the son of the Jehovah's Witness (still attending at age 20) and the Anglican's daughter. The distinguishing feature in each case was that their fathers attended as regularly and frequently as their mothers, unlike the fathers of the other children in the three schools.

108

Table 6.4
'Religion is something which children have to make up their own minds about': attitudes of mothers when child age 10/11 by school

	Penvollard Church school %	Penvollard County school %
Agree Strongly	29	57
Agree	41	21
Agree but need guidance when young	24	14
Disagree	06	07
	100	100
(N)	(18)	(14)

None of the other mothers set a particular age for children to make a decision about religion but one, who had been to various denominations herself having been brought up as a Catholic, made it clear that having given the 'guidelines' she 'would not be worried if they became a Buddhist or another religion'. For her the important thing was for them 'to have a belief in the good'. Other mothers who went to church regularly or occasionally felt children should 'make up their own minds' about religion but none of them rated religion as more than 'fairly important'. Mothers seemed more likely to encourage boys to attend a church rather than girls, as already discussed. All the mothers had more than one child and many had both boys and girls. In none of these families did a boy go but not his sister whereas several mothers mentioned that a daughter still went or went longer than a son, especially to Sunday school.

'It is important for children to go to a church or Sunday school'

The mothers' feelings that children should not be unduly influenced in religious matters and that churchgoing is particularly appropriate for young children were again revealed. A majority of mothers disagreed with the statement in both Penvollard schools and a quarter of them added spontaneously that children 'should not be forced' or 'only if they want to'. These mothers wanted to stress that the decision should lie with their children, some of whom did attend and some of whom did not. About a quarter of the mothers made comments about churchgoing as particularly suitable for primary age children and assumed that older children would not want to attend. At the second interview a few more mothers in Penvollard Church school agreed with the statement as they looked back to when their children were younger;

I liked mine to go when they were younger.

I don't manage to make it work with mine, did [go] when they were young enough.

It's good for them to learn about Bible stories, part of their upbringing. But you can have too much religion especially if you don't believe in it.

The four mothers who had disagreed with the previous statement and felt children *should* be guided in religious matters, might have been expected to agree with this one, since they were all practising members of their churches. In fact they were divided. The two whose children still attended a church agreed that it was important for children to do so, but the other two said children could not and should not be forced, presumably because they had been unable or unwilling to force their own children to go.

'The churches have little influence or importance these days'

Most mothers did not have regular contact with a local church. Mothers who went regularly to church were most likely to disagree with the statement and those who never attended were most likely to agree with it. Overall those with children at church aided schools saw the church as having more influence than those with children at the county school . Around half the mothers agreed with statement and most of them felt the church had less influence than it used to have and that this was unfortunate. One regular churchgoer had changed her mind from the first interview because 'wonderful things have happened' and mentioned some of them; 'all the fuss about the Bishop of Durham, Terry Waite, the Church's report on the inner cities, the grave distrust of the government for the Church of England ... '.

Among the children, girls were a little more likely to agree with the statement than boys (33 per cent: 24 per cent) but nearly as many were uncertain (23 per cent). Some made the distinction between older and younger people, as one girl put it ' it depends who with, with older people it still has importance but with younger people not really'. It might have been expected that girls, who are more likely to attend a church regularly, would disagree with the statement. However among both the boys and the girls most of those who were not involved in a church at all and whose families were not involved, disagreed with the statement. They made comments like; 'no, they have a lot of importance' or 'there are still a lot of religious people about' or 'a lot of people go to church and enjoy it'. The children were thinking in terms of whether people go to church, and they knew a lot of people still did go, whereas their mothers tended to be referring to the influence of the church on the wider society.

Attitudes to religion in school

Bible reading and knowledge

In their last year at primary school the children were much more likely than their mothers to say that they read the Bible regularly with no gender differences (40 per cent of both boys and girls). But by 12/13, while the percentage of girls reading the Bible remained steady only one boy, from the Jehovah's Witness family, still claimed to do so. The girls who attended Junior Church at the Methodist chapel were given a Bible when they moved into the seniors class (for ages eleven to fifteen) and encouraged to read it using notes supplied. Pathfinders, the Anglican Church's group for the same age range also gave children a Bible when they moved up from Sunday school. Since boys were less likely to attend these groups this may have accounted for the decline in Bible reading among boys.

Knowledge of Bible stories was influenced more by the school attended than by churchgoing, and gender was not significant. The importance of school was also shown when children were asked if they had a favourite Bible story and where they had first heard it. All but one had heard it first at school either in religious education or in an assembly. The greater number of girls naming a favourite story probably reflected their more positive attitudes to religion.

Penvollard Church school based its religious education syllabus firmly on the Bible and children there scored highest on knowledge out of the three schools. Nearly half the children at Penvollard Church school had a high score and only one child had a low score. The school was therefore successful in inculcating knowledge even in the boys who were generally less positive in their attitudes to religion, although the girls tended to give fuller answers. The differences in scores could not be explained by the child's attendance at church or Sunday school because some children who never attended scored the highest marks in all three schools. At Penvollard county school knowledge of Bible stories was generally lower than in the Church school among both boy and girls, despite the fact that girls but not boys attended the Methodist Sunday school. Over a third had a low score. Both Penvollard county school and the village Church school stressed 'caring' in their religious education syllabuses but the village Church school had Christian assemblies with readings from the Bible. Children there occupied a middle position, none knew all the answers but they tended to know more than those in the county school.

Religious assemblies

More mothers had changed their attitude to statements on religious education and assemblies between the interviews, than on any other topic.

The reason seemed to be that their children were older and the type of religious education and assemblies had changed as they moved from primary to secondary school. The practice at the comprehensive school attended by most of their children was to have one full assembly a week, for the whole of the lower school, taken by the headmaster and including a hymn and prayers, and a weekly year group assembly with notices. All the primary schools had daily assemblies which, according to the headmasters, were to worship God in both church schools and to teach the 'ethic of Christianity' in the county school. Mothers were aware of the change in the type of assembly, particularly from the church schools where parents had had the opportunity to go to assemblies weekly in Penvollard Church school and to regular church services in both schools. The statement 'it is important to have religious assemblies [everyday] at school' revealed that such assemblies were seen as particularly appropriate for young children. At the first interview assemblies had been generally accepted as part of school. The most frequent rider to agreeing with the statement was 'it doesn't do them any harm'. By the second interview when the children were older fewer mothers thought it did children any good either, a change from;

> I agree, it doesn't hurt them for ten minutes or quarter of an hour ... [to] ... not as they get older. James is starting to rebel [about churchgoing], his sort of age is quite difficult.

Although the statement on religious assemblies was put in general terms all the children answered in relation to their experience at school, as did their parents. This was the statement with the lowest level of agreement between mothers and children, due to the views of the boys. Forty one per cent of boys chose 'no particular opinion' as their view on the statement, compared with only seven per cent of girls and five per cent of mothers. Some of these boys were, perhaps, politely disagreeing as they added that assemblies were 'boring', they 'had never liked them' or 'they are just another lesson', comments that were also made by the 36 per cent of boys who disagreed with the statement. Just over half the girls disagreed with the statement and tended to focus on both their boredom and their physical discomfort in the once a week religious assembly. One girl said 'we have to stand up, [I] have aching legs. I got a detention for talking ... I told the girl next to me I was squashed'. Another girl interviewed the day after such an assembly commented;

> I couldn't hear very well. I was behind the benches. I did know the hymn - I don't usually know the hymns. [Assemblies] were better at [Penvollard Church] school.

None of the children had taken part in more than one or two assemblies in the two years they had been there. When they were at primary school Penvollard Church school children were more enthusiastic about their religious assemblies than Penvollard Junior school children, whereas they were less likely to agree that religious assemblies were important at secondary school (17 per cent Penvollard Church school: 46 per cent Penvollard junior). Their enthusiasm had been for the type of assemblies they had at primary school, in which they were regularly involved, acting, miming or reading Children described assemblies they had helped to devise, dramatising a Bible story or a modern story with a moral theme.

Of the children who agreed that it was important to have religious assemblies over half had no contact with a church. They tended also to agree with the statement that 'religious education is an important part of our education' and to disagree with the view that 'the churches have little importance or influence these days'.

Religious Education

Overall the mothers answers showed an acceptance of religious education in schools, teaching both Christianity and 'other religions' but were divided on whether religious education was also moral education (table 6:5).

Table 6.5
Statements on religious education: agreement of mothers by school
(%)

	Village Church school	Penvollard Church school	Penvollard County junior
Children ought to know about Christianity	100	100	100
RE teaches children about right and wrong	100	56	43
RE is an important part of children's education	100	72	64

The most general statement was 'religious education is an important part of children's education' with which only 10 per cent of mothers simply disagreed, none of whom were at the village Church school (table 6.5). However over half the mothers with children at Penvollard Church school made adverse comments about the amount of time spent on religious education, not because they felt religion should not come into school but because it should not interfere with other aspects of education. In the next

113

section, the mothers indicate some of the reasons why they chose a church school (see p. 117) . Comments on religious education included;

> It was a bit overdone sometimes. I would like more attention to reading writing and arithmetic.
> The religious side is so heavy it's unrealistic.
> You've got to draw a happy medium as to how much you do in RE.
> At [Penvollard Church school] it was too important.

Whereas the mothers who made those comments found that RE. became 'just another subject' at the comprehensive school, most of the Penvollard county school mothers were surprised by how much attention it was given in terms of time in class (three hours of RE a fortnight in years 1-3) and the regular homework.

As with other attitude questions girls were more likely to have a definite opinion on the statement 'religious education is an important part of our education' than boys. Only one girl was unsure compared with nearly a third of the boys. Because of the large group of boys choosing 'no particular opinion', girls were both more likely to agree and to disagree with the statement than boys. Answers were related to church attendance with only 13 per cent of regular churchgoers disagreeing with the statement compared to 41 per cent of non-churchgoers. Among those attending less regularly the numbers agreeing and disagreeing were equal.

Looking at the content of religious education, the statement; 'children ought to learn about Christianity as part of our country's heritage', was the only one which received unanimous support among mothers at both interviews (table 6:5). In contrast, only 60 per cent of children agreed that they should learn about Christianity in school and although girls were much more likely still to attend a church at 12/13 years old, fewer of them agreed with the statement than boys. Children might be resistant to any suggestion of what they 'ought to learn' but when asked whether they should be taught about non-Christian religions, which all of them had been in secondary school, only 13 per cent of children disagreed.

When the children were at primary school only those in the village church school had learnt anything about non-Christian religion but 77 per cent of mothers agreed with the statement 'children should be taught about different religions, other than Christianity, at school'. By the second interview, when their children were older, only two of these mothers still disagreed. Religious education was seen by most mothers as a factual subject, teaching children about other people's beliefs in order to make up their own minds. It has already been seen that mothers emphasised that their children should have autonomy in religious matters. A Penvollard county school mother illustrates this in her comment on the teaching of non-Christian religions to her daughter;

I agree now she is old enough ... do different religions at school and I see that she can take it, not the younger one. If she decided to change her religion to different beliefs, fine.

Religious education in schools has been associated with moral education. The 1964 Cornwall agreed syllabus was in use until 1971, a period when most of the mothers would have been at school. It was based on a study of the Bible (Cornwall County Council, 1964). It had a course entitled Christian conduct described as 'a preparation of the pupils for life in the world when schooldays are over', seeking to help children to lead a Christian life not just to learn about how Christians live. The three primary schools and Penvollard comprehensive school in the lower school, all emphasised moral education. At Penvollard comprehensive religious education became part of 'social, moral and personal education' from age 14 for those not taking a GCSE in the subject. It might be assumed, therefore, that parental support for religious education is partly based on the hope that it will make children good, a view certainly shared by many who took part in the Parliamentary debate on the 1988 Education Reform Act (chapter 3). The statement 'religious education teaches children about right and wrong' was intended to see whether the mothers did equate religious with moral education and if their views changed when their children moved from primary to secondary school.

At the first interview, when their children were at primary school, mothers with children in a Church school were most likely to agree with the statement. They assumed that religious education was teaching Christian values, a 'guide to life', a valid assumption given the Church school syllabuses. Only one mother simply disagreed and the rest wanted to qualify the statement to say that 'other things do that as well'. The unanimous agreement among village Church school mothers seemed to be due to their high opinion of the local Rector, Father Mark, who took their children for religious education and, in his own words, tried to animate them in the Christian faith. By the second interview, with their children at secondary school, most of the village school mothers had changed their minds and were unsure whether religious education taught about right and wrong because they no longer knew what their children did in religious education. In Penvollard county school only 40 per cent agreed with the statement and most of them qualified their agreement adding 'it should do' or 'I suppose it does really on the whole'. One mother 'agreed strongly' having already said that 'the [Christian] way of bringing up children [is] important'. Those who disagreed included the Witness mother who equated religion and morality but did not like the type of teaching in state schools.

There was little unqualified equation of religious with moral education. The comments mothers made seem to fall into three categories. Firstly, the mothers did not have 'blind faith' that any religious education taught by anyone would teach their children about right and wrong. One mother pointed out that religious education 'teaches them about the Bible and that's not necessarily about right and wrong'. However once her son was at the comprehensive school she agreed with the statement because 'they have different RE now, more about modern things'. Others whose children had been at a church school felt that religious education had given moral guidance there but not to the same extent at secondary school. Secondly, mothers said that religious education alone could not teach morality and parents had a more important role. Children could learn right and wrong at school but that would not necessarily make them moral because it needed to be part of everyday life;

> Up to the parents to do that using religion as an example, not
> leaving it solely to religion to teach them. [They] can learn right
> and wrong at school and still do wrong. Parents and the way you are
> brought up teaches you that. You can learn it at home.

Other comments were 'home life is more important'; 'religious education 'helps but parents have more influence' and 'religion can be too idealistic'. The third category consisted of comments which stressed the difficulty or impossibility of teaching morality and the need to consider the child as an individual. Teaching morality in schools implies a body of knowledge which can be given to all children but modern mothers expect children to question received knowledge as they have done themselves, and make up their own minds. One mother gave her relativistic view of morality;

> I think if you take it from the Bible there is right and wrong in it but
> it's not always a good example. They have to learn for themselves
> what is right for them and wrong for them. You can't say what is
> right for them and wrong for them. You can't say what is right for
> somebody is right for you, it might be wrong for you.

This mother gave a more extended comment on something assumed by other mothers who simply said 'it depends on what you think is right and wrong, what you believe in, it's personal' or 'the child interprets what is taught'. The view that children must not just be inculcated with beliefs seen as desirable by adults is one which occurs again in mothers' comments on the desirability of children going to church and Sunday school. The children were less likely than their mothers to agree that religious education teaches about right and wrong but girls were at least twice as likely to agree as boys in each school. Those who added comments tended to point out the sort of things they actually learned in religious education at their schools.

Differences between Penvollard schools

Perhaps because Penvollard Church school was oversubscribed parents whose children attended were more conscious of the differences between the school and other local schools. Most of those with children at Penvollard county junior said there were no particular differences and the remaining four mentioned only that the county school was smaller. In contrast over 80 per cent of Penvollard Church school mothers gave between one and four differences.

Table 6.6
Mothers' perceptions of the differences between Penvollard Church and county junior schools

	Church school	County junior school
No differences (%)	18	71
Number of mentions	**Church school**	**County junior school**
RE/Assemblies	10	0
Family atmosphere	5	0
Social differences	4	0
Modern facilities	4	0
Christian ethos/staff	4	0
School size	0	4
Discipline & manners	3	0

Table 6.7
Mothers' perceptions of the differences between their child's primary school and Penvollard secondary school*

Penvollard Church school mothers	Penvollard County junior mothers
Social differences	School size
RE/Assemblies	More discipline
Less academic push	Different teachers/subjects
Bigger school/less family atmosphere	
Less discipline	

*Differences chosen by 25 per cent or more of mothers who replied; in order of preference

117

Although a greater emphasis on religious education and assemblies was mentioned most often by the mothers at Penvollard Church school it became apparent that this was not what had attracted them to the school. In fact over 40 per cent of mothers specifically criticised the amount of time spent or the emphasis given to religion at some time during the first interview. When Church school mothers were asked about the purpose of the Church of England's involvement in primary education all those who answered said something about providing Christian education or education on Church of England lines. Therefore mothers were expecting an emphasis on Christianity but not the type or the amount of time given to it. Putting together the comments on differences between Penvollard Church school, other primary schools and the comprehensive school, mothers did approve of the family atmosphere, discipline, manners and academic standards of the Church school and worried that these might be reduced in the secondary school (tables 6:6 and 6:7. The mothers were also aware of the social differences between Penvollard schools but tended to acknowledge these rather than directly approve of them. Typical comments from three mothers were;

> She will mix with a wider range of children. I know there will be much more disturbed behaviour in the classroom than is tolerated at [Penvollard Church school].
> Far more professional people at [Penvollard Church school].
> From a small family atmosphere he will meet tougher boys.

Conclusion

Very few of the children came from 'Christian homes' in the sense of homes where both parents were practising Christians but none came from atheist homes either. Many of the organised activities available to children still had a church or chapel connection and this involvement in children's and youth work was accepted as legitimate by the families. The families lived in a small market town over twenty miles from any large urban centre where they were unlikely to have personal contact with members of non-Christian religions. However parents and children were aware that Christian belief is only one option and rarely features as part of youth culture on television programmes, in popular music or magazines. The central values which emerged from the mothers' answers to questions on religion were a stress on individual autonomy concerning religious matters and apparent tolerance of religion. However the tolerance was only of normal levels of religion, not of excessive churchgoing, excessive religious education or public display which might be seen as intruding on other people's autonomy.

Christianity was accepted as a desirable part of being very young. It was pre-school and in the early years of primary school that the largest proportion of children attended a church. Nativity plays, assemblies and Bible stories were seen as particularly appropriate for young children, both by their mothers and by the children, when they were older themselves.

Church activities had to compete with other activities which attracted children after school and at weekends, a range of activities which would not have been open to earlier generations in a rural area. Most children who did attend a church or chapel went without an adult and so were usually restricted to one within walking distance and with special provision for their age group. Girls were more likely than boys to participate in any organised social activities, apart from sport, both inside and outside school. Once churchgoing became a voluntary activity the appeal of the activity to the individual child, rather than to the parents, was the crucial factor. The various junior churches in Penvollard attracted more girls than boys and all involved similar activities; reading, writing and drawing and opportunities for acting and singing. Both boys and girls engage in these activities at school but girls tend to dominate those which are voluntary, for example, school recorder groups and choirs. Girls had more favourable attitudes to religion and the church than boys, rather than greater knowledge of Christianity. Whether these attitudes were due to attendance at a junior church or to the example of their mothers, they seem likely to be one factor in the higher levels of adult attendance among women compared with men. None of the boys had fathers who attended more than their mothers and they would be aware that junior churches and congregations are predominantly female [1].

Children were not yet associating religion with hypocrisy, unlike their mothers. They saw churches and clergy as resources available to anyone who wanted them and which people ought to know about in order to make their own decisions about religion. Whereas the mothers had been brought up to go to church the only compulsion for their children now came from school, with compulsory religious education and, in the church schools, daily religious assemblies. Children had less personal experience of religion than their mothers, thought less about it and had lower levels of belief. Whether this would change as the children grew up remains to be seen. The contribution of primary school was difficult to assess. Penvollard Church schoolchildren had gained Bible knowledge from the Bible based syllabus and a positive attitude towards the Church school assemblies but not to religion or Christianity in general. Religious attitudes and attitudes to religious education were more clearly related to church attendance and gender than to attendance of a church school.

Notes

1   Cornwall churchgoers were 39 per cent male and 61 per cent female according to a survey based on responses from 70 per cent of all churches in Cornwall (Brierley, 1991b, p.25). In the Cornish population as a whole the percentages of men and women are equal until the 45-64 age group in which women exceed men by one per cent and the 65 and over group in which women exceed men by three per cent.

Postscript

A Catholic primary school

The same interviews were carried out with a sample of seven families from the nearest Catholic primary school to Penvollard. As discussed in chapter 4, Catholic schools tend to have a stronger denominational identity than Anglican schools and provide a Catholic education for Catholic families. Like Penvollard Church school, the Catholic school provided an alternative to the county school but according to the handbooks, Penvollard Church school offered 'an alternative choice of a Christian based education', whereas the Catholic school aimed 'to provide for the Catholic families of the area a school whose ethos would be that of the Catholic Christian home'. The admission policy was based solely on denominational criteria at the Catholic school. All Catholic children, children of Catholic parents and those coming from other Catholic schools would be accepted. Only if there was still room would non-Catholic children 'whose parents want a Christian education' be considered. In the year 6 class (age 10-11) there were Catholic children who were baptised and had had first communion and others who came from non-Catholic or non-practising Catholic families. This information was included on the school register, whereas at the Anglican Church schools the headteacher claimed to have 'no idea' of children's religious background or practice. The influence of the school could be compared with the other church schools because most of the children went on to an ordinary comprehensive school. Like Penvollard Church school the Catholic school was oversubscribed and was seen as a good school in the town which had two other primary schools, one Anglican and one county school.

The low level of Catholicism in Cornwall has already been commented on and none of the Catholics in the sample were born in Cornwall (p. 66). Looking at the current religious practice of the families, the pattern was one of regular attendance by children who were baptised and their Catholic parent or parents, and no involvement in the Catholic Church by the other families. The occasional churchgoing found in Penvollard Church school and attendance of children at Sunday school was absent. Children either attended with an adult or did not go at all. This may have accounted for the stability of churchgoing. None of the children 'dropped out' between the two interviews nor had any of them attended more regularly in the past. They did not grow out of Church unlike the children who grew out of Sunday school. Whereas in the other schools confirmation was left up to the child, all the Catholic schoolchildren who were baptised were confirmed or preparing for confirmation by age 12/13. The two Catholic fathers married to non-Catholics were the only men out of the forty three families interviewed to attend more regularly than their wives. Nationally the Roman Catholic Church does have a higher proportion of men than the Methodist and Anglican Churches (Brierley, 1991a, p.85)

Looking for any contrasts with the other schools one obvious one was that children from the Catholic school had the lowest score on Bible knowledge. The results seemed to reflect the programme of religious education which stressed values and attitudes rather than knowledge, as the headmistress explained;

> Too much knowledge can be a bad thing. I don't like Bible stories, miracles I handle carefully.[it is] what is underlying the stories that is important. (Sister D)

All the mothers commented on the relationships within the school and the care taken with each child, including the special needs children who were taught in a separate class. The school's statement on religious education began with the aim;

> To share faith with all children by extending and clarifying their experience of faith (1) by introducing them to the source of revelation (2) by relating God's message to their present lives and by the example of the lives of faith we ourselves live.

Mothers accepted the emphasis on Christianity whether or not they were practising Christians themselves. None of the mothers expressed reservations about the amount of time spent on religion or complained of 'indoctrination' unlike the mothers in Penvollard Church school. The official view of the role of Church of England schools sees them as 'caring' communities but it was the Catholic school that was most often experienced as such with all the mothers mentioning some aspect of 'caring'. One mother from Penvollard Church school made an explicit contrast between it and the Catholic school her son had previously attended when they lived in Devon;

The Roman Catholic school had a feeling for community and other people as human beings ... consideration for others.

The practice of Catholicism was built into the life of the school to a greater extent than in the Anglican schools. There were weekly masses and preparation for first communion, as well as Sunday masses which children took part in at the local church. Whether the mothers were Catholic or not they all agreed that religious education was an important part of education and were more likely than those from other schools to agree that it taught children about right and wrong, adding that the whole school helped to teach moral values. Comments from five of the mothers illustrate their positive view of the school's ethos;

When they go to [Catholic school] they are influenced just by being there. I hope it stays with them ... (Non-RC mother)
[The school] is like a family ... felt cared for there. (Non-RC mother)
I feel it has a much more caring atmosphere between the staff and pupils and between the pupils themselves ... a lovely atmosphere. (RC mother)
They are always praising one another, no jealousy ... comradeship [The children] delight in someone doing well. They are good with disabled children. (RC convert mother)
The school is quite helpful to single parents. (Non-RC mother)

Both Penvollard Church school and the Catholic school invited parents to a weekly assembly, which was a mass at the Catholic school. There was none of the criticism of assemblies or religious education which was expressed in Penvollard Church school, although the time spent on them and the confessional approach was similar. Perhaps mothers knew what to expect from a Catholic school whereas Anglican schools vary considerably and several mothers specifically said they were surprised by the emphasis on religion at Penvollard Church school.

The mothers from the Catholic school said they were 'fairly religious' and then distanced themselves from a 'narrow' or 'bigoted' faith, described by one Catholic mother as 'accept[ing] all that the Church says, the old fashioned Catholic thing'. This was a rather different view of the undesirable aspects of religion from the mothers at other schools since it focused on the belief rather than ostentatious display. However there was the same rejection of missionary work in the community, when mothers were asked to rate the importance of different aspects of religion. It was important to act as a Christian by being a good neighbour but not by going to church or performing any other public act reflecting specific faith rather than general humanitarianism. On the other hand the mothers were less

122

rejecting of the public aspects of religiosity than those in other schools. Only two mothers, with no church connections, did not agree that it was important for children to go to church, whereas in Penvollard Church school a majority disagreed. The view prevalent in other schools, that children should only go willingly was not relevant to the Catholic school because none of the children attended a Sunday school. Instead they either went with the rest of the family or did not go at all. The Catholic school mothers were also the most likely to disagree with the view that the churches now have little influence or importance. These more positive attitudes may have been connected to the mothers' perception of the school as conveying the humanitarian values which they felt were the most important part of being religious while at the same time having a strong basis in the Catholic faith and practice which was not forced on the children. Comments included;

> Values are important ... caring and discipline are good. The children respect it and they love the Sisters ...
> A true Christian attitude like [the Catholic school] ... a community beneficial to children.

Another reason for the mothers' support for the school was the sense that children need to be protected from the world outside and worries about the more 'open' approach to religion at the comprehensive school. Some Penvollard Church school mothers referred to the more sheltered life at the school compared with the comprehensive but their worries were about the social rather than the religious characteristics of the school.

At the age of 16/17 all the children who had been practising Catholics continued to attend with their families, but two did not attend as regularly as before. The pattern was the same as the other three schools in that the children still attending at 16/17 were the children whose fathers had been as regular in attendance as their mothers. Changes in churchgoing would perhaps occur when the 'children' left home and the pattern of family attendance was broken.

7 The future for 'normal' religion

> We were brought up to go to church and I feel guilty if I don't go but Stephanie was not brought up to it - it's different for them.

What does 'normal' religion consist of? For the mother quoted above it is a residual feeling of guilt, but not enough to make her ever attend a church, and a determination not to force her own children to attend but to leave it up to them. She believed in God and agreed that religious education was part of education but said it was 'not an important part'. All but two of the mothers in this study had been 'brought up to it', going to Church, or more usually Sunday school, regularly in childhood. Most then ceased to attend as they grew up and felt strongly that their children should not be pressurised into churchgoing.

When studying a small town like Penvollard it is easy to look at the past, perhaps with nostalgia, as a time when there was a strong sense of shared values in a community which was stable and had its roots in the land; when young people had not yet got 'the spirit of wandering' on Sunday afternoons and the certainties of the Christian faith were taught in school and Sunday school. In fact the history of the Penvollard area shows a rather more complicated picture. The local population may now be diluted by incomers from other parts of Britain but in the last century miners flooded in, particularly from Ireland, and the population was about the same as it was in the 1990s before falling dramatically as employment declined. The more recent incomers are attracted by the rural environment of Cornwall and prepared to commute for work or set up their own businesses. In the past people had little choice over where they lived and social events were necessarily local, but, by the 1980s and 1990s choice and individual autonomy were valued although the opportunities to exercise them is still related to social and economic circumstances. Neither does the religious map of Penvollard look stable. In the last century Methodist groups split and merged and a Roman Catholic Church was built to accommodate migrant workers, as described in chapter 5. At the end of the

125

twentieth century there is no simple pattern of decline; the Jehovah's Witness congregation continues to expand and a new Methodist breakaway group attracts congregations of 200, while the original group continues. In a small town of around 7000 there are eleven varieties of Christianity to choose from, with additional choices in the surrounding area for those with cars, including an Anglo-Catholic Church and Baptist chapel.

The Anglican and Methodist Churches still provided services to young children which most families in Penvollard used; most children were baptised, all children attended services with their primary school and the local clergy visited all the schools. Nothing was required of the parents in return. In contrast the Christian groups which are growing in Penvollard make demands on their members in terms of behaviour and beliefs. The Witnesses disfellowship those who do not conform to their standards. They, and the Independent Churches offer certainty of belief and control of lifestyle. There is thus a polarization between the 'normal' religion of the majority and the religion of the committed.

While government advisers for schools, with support from the traditionalists whose views were described in chapter 3, condemn 'moral relativism' and argue that schools should 'pass on the personal values that had been accepted without question by previous generations' (Dr. Nicholas Tate, School Curriculum and Assessment Authority, Telegraph, 16.1.96) the majority of mothers considered values in relation to the situation in which their children were growing up. The idea that education would teach a set of moral truths was not subscribed to by these mothers, as the following comments from three different mothers illustrate;

> I hope her education will equip her to assess things and work out what she believes ...
> [there is a] danger of children echoing their parents ... [I want her to] work out life in general for herself ... I want her to make up her own mind [about values].
> I try to give them information without bias ... get different views not just mine ... I have my own private views ...

The nominally Christian had a strong sense that right and wrong had to be worked out by an individual for him or herself. Individual autonomy involved the right to question and the nominally Christian mothers did not subscribe to one moral authority. The mothers appeared to be expressing a child-centred view of education but at the same time most of the Church school parents had chosen the school for its reputation as a good school, with traditional education and orderliness. Certainly religious beliefs were an optional extra and in that area the right to question was supreme but perhaps not the right to a strong faith. One mother who had attended

126

Penvollard grammar school (now a comprehensive and attended by her children) looked back on her own religious education;

> We were sat there and RE was drummed in ... Bible stories. There wasn't the communication, children were not allowed their views. They have the right to question and to ask about any aspects of religion or whatever they don't understand or can't cope with.

Changes in religious education fit in with the values expressed by these mothers. Since 1944, religious education in schools has changed from a subject assumed to be taught by Christian teachers and aiming to make children into Christians, to multi-cultural religious education aiming to teach tolerance and empathy for the variety of faiths in Britain. These values are becoming official school policy embodied in equal opportunities statements and in action against gender and racial discrimination, some of the policies being backed by law. Thus multi-cultural religious education fits in with other aspects of school life and with wider social values such as respect for the individual. In theory the changes are not relevant to Church aided schools because religious education and worship in those schools are bound by their Trust deed. In practice the provision in Church of England schools tends to resemble that in other maintained schools, and recent Diocesan syllabuses and Church of England reports emphasise the same values of toleration, caring and respect for the faith of the individual.

The mother who experienced RE at Penvollard grammar had changed her opinion of it having seen the multicultural RE taught at the comprehensive school. In response to the statement 'Religious education is an important part of children's education' she said;

> I don't think [religious education] is very important but attitudes have changed in RE enough for me not to disagree. I could only go by my teaching last time.

Although parents are primarily attracted by the social and academic reputation of church schools, this includes the general Christian ethos, with values of caring and a 'feeling of family' which are in accord with mainstream societal values. There had been major changes in the content and structure of education since the parents were in school, including the National Curriculum and GCSEs but RE and assemblies were both familiar and accepted as a continuing part of education so long as they did not interfere with other more important aspects of education. Parents saw Christianity as particularly appropriate for young children; the traditional celebrations of harvest, Christmas and Easter are a familiar and desirable part of childhood. In a survey carried out by the Independent in 1993, half

127

the parents wanted their children to be taught that the Bible is true (Independent, 6.9.93). Since the percentage claiming to hold that belief themselves is lower, it seems to be on a par with parents wanting their young children to believe in Father Christmas - parents ask each other as Christmas approaches, does he/she still believe? By which they mean, not does the child believe in the Christian stories about Jesus but does he/she believe in Father Christmas. It is part of the innocence of childhood. However, at Penvollard Church school the headteacher aimed to teach a more complete version of Christianity, not just the 'nice bits'. This was not seen as so suitable for young children. A mother talked about religion at Penvollard Church school;

> It's not a bad thing with Nicholas's age group ... Nicholas has got opinions by ten, it washes over them, they don't take it so seriously. The mum is concerned next door, she has younger children.

The aspects of religion which they particularly disliked were the idea that churchgoing people are better in a moral sense, any attempt to indoctrinate children or force religious ideas on other people and the suggestion that children should go to a church or Sunday school. The continuing popularity of Anglican schools owes much to the combination of a wary approach to Christian witness and an embracing of the values of toleration and caring.

Penvollard Church school was an atypical Church school which under the influence of its founding headmaster developed a more overtly Christian stance. Unlike Catholic schools it did not have a strong denominational identity; there were no Eucharistic services or confirmation classes in school nor were assemblies or classroom religious education specifically Anglican. Most of the mothers nevertheless felt their values to be threatened. Although many of them claimed that they wanted their children to 'make up their own minds' about values a strong commitment to religion was not expected. Mothers who had a loose affiliation to the Church of England and attended occasionally expected the Church's schools to be open to their children, if they wanted them to attend, but did not feel any particular obligations to the Church.

It is often assumed that those with a residual faith will turn to it again in times of crisis. In the course of the research six of the mothers had such crises: deaths in the family, divorce, serious illness or problems with a child. All of them said it had made them think about God but only those who already had a church connection turned to a particular church. However, rather than their faith being increased it was more often diminished. One woman said she was no longer sure about the existence of God because 'when things happen to you, you think it wouldn't have happened if there was a God'. and another reported that she had no answer when her son asked why his granddad had died, because he had been a good man but evil people seem to flourish. Others were disappointed with the reaction of people in the church to their problems. When it came to a crisis their residual faith, instilled in childhood, had no answers or comfort. They asked the basic questions all religions consider; why do the innocent suffer?, why do we have to die?, as a criticism of the churches, not seeking answers. To borrow from Alasdair MacIntyre, they may have lost their capacity to use, or listen to religious language (MacIntyre, 1981, p.2). The nice bits of religion which they wanted for their children did not seem much help when life threw up nasty things. The mothers' lives revolved around their families. All those who worked, whatever their social class, had jobs that fitted around the children; primary school teaching, part time nursing, school dinner supervising, part time work in a shop, working in the family business. When things went wrong in the family religion did not help the nominally Christian.

What sort of God do the normally or nominally Christian believe in? Not an aweful or mysterious God but something waiting undemandingly in the background and, when called upon, found to be rather disappointing. The mothers felt able to call on God because they identified themselves as 'fairly religious' (religious being synonymous with Christianity). They felt that they followed the important aspects of Christianity, the moral and social aspects rather than going to church every Sunday.

Their children had experienced religion as an optional activity out of school. They did not associate religious practice with hypocrisy, but simply saw it as something some people like to do. Given the changes in RE in schools and the attitudes of their mothers they might not have the same residual association of Christian with morality and thus no reason to claim any allegiance to Christianity when they reached adulthood. Osmond's recent study, based on a Gallup survey which excluded those from non-Christian faiths, provides evidence of the decline in the significance of Christianity and the prevalence of individualistic values (Osmond, 1993). Nearly half the student sample 'strongly agreed' that 'the main purpose in life is to fulfil yourself, and another 40 per cent 'tended to agree' (Osmond, 1993, p.14). Perhaps pointing the way to the answers of the Cornish children in a few years time, the students were significantly less likely than the older people in the sample to say that their private life fitted in with Christian morality (59 per cent: 91 per cent.) (Osmond, 1993, p. 84).

If present trends continue the daughters in this survey will have any children later than their mothers did and will work for a higher proportion of their lives. They had been encouraged to believe that they should (and could) do what they want to do and might be in a more equal partnership than their mothers in terms of the balance of work and family. Most had not yet encountered the crises which had made some of the mothers reassess their religiosity but when such crises did occur would they be likely to see mainstream religion as in any way relevant? It was not part of daily life or popular culture, its rituals were not built into family life and elements of practice were left behind with primary school. Imbued with the ideology of individualism perhaps the self help approach will appeal more to their generation, selecting from among New Age beliefs as the need arises. At the other extreme, the evangelical Christian groups also focus on the individual but require a great deal more commitment. Although their missionary activity and public statements of faith were anathema to the mothers their children were starting with less religious baggage. In Penvollard these groups tended to attract people from other churches or the 'lapsed' but will need to broaden their appeal if they are to maintain numbers in the future.

The mainstream Christian churches attract the under 8's and women in disproportionate numbers. Mothers, rather than fathers, tend to have the greater part in the socialization of young children, and religion is still seen as a normal part of childhood. If young women, like those in Penvollard, do not take on the traditional family role of their mothers then their religious practice and beliefs, and those of their children, may become closer to the male pattern, with lower rates of churchgoing and higher rates of atheism.

Uncertainty about religion was not a problem for nominal Christians; certainty would have been as it might require some sort of activity beyond the 'normal' level. The four women who practised a religion were both certain about their beliefs and expressed them publicly to varying degrees. The nominally Christian kept their religion private and expected others to do the same.

Appendix 1
Case studies of four 'religious' women and their families

These case studies of mothers and children from four families have been chosen not because they were typical but because they were the only families in which the mother went to a religious service every week. When churchgoing was more common this might not have been significant but these mothers were distinctive in their attitudes as well. They stood apart with different answers to the other mothers on the question 'how important is religion in your life' and the statement 'religion is something children have to make up their own minds about'. For these mothers religion was 'very important' and they saw their role as guiding children when young by encouraging religious practice so that they could make up their own minds later on. Two of the mothers said the children did not have a choice over whether or not to attend because the whole family did so and a child of 10/11 would not be left alone. The other two mothers had husbands who were not Christians, one of whom never attended and one who went occasionally. The children, three boys and two girls including a twin boy and girl, were churchgoers at the first interview but by age 16/17 only two children continued to attend regularly. They were the children who attended with the whole family rather than with their mothers or other children. Two of the families were contacted in 1996 to bring the case studies up to date but the other two had moved from the area.

Case 1 An Anglican family

Susan is from a professional background. Her father is a scientist and her mother also has a science degree. Her mother had enrolled on a postgraduate teaching course at the first interview and was teaching in a nearby primary school by the second interview. She had started training as a lay reader but gave it up temporarily while she settled into full time work.

She was asked by the Rector to be a governor of Penvollard Church school when it first opened and Susan later attended the school.

Susan went to the Anglican Church every week with her mother, brother and sister and her father when he was home. Her brother and sister both enjoyed the Church groups for young people, Pathfinders and Cyfa which they still attended at the first interview (aged 17 and 14). Susan went to youth club at Church and Guides. She was confirmed when she was thirteen.

For her mother religion is 'very much part of life' and 'very important'. The headteacher of her primary school and the head of RE at her comprehensive school attended the same Anglican Church. She was in the top set for one subject at Penvollard comprehensive, religious education. For Susan, home, school and church seem to be congruent but, unlike the older children in her family, she was hostile to church although she did not show the same opposition in the attitude questions. For example, she agreed with the statement; 'there are some mysteries in life that science can never explain' and agreed that Christianity and other religions should be taught in school. She said she did not know if there is a God but she did think about what God might be like;

> Is he really as powerful as everyone thinks? I think he's sort of behind the sun ... in the rays of the sun ...

Unlike her mother, she agreed that 'religion is something children should make up their own minds about'. Her opposition was to the religious practice insisted upon by her mother. She wanted to leave Guides but said 'mum won't let me' and got confirmed 'before mum could go on about it'. She went to Pathfinders because she had to and her mother said the older children 'couldn't understand it when she said she didn't want to go because they loved it'. This was confirmed by the older girl, aged 17, who still enjoyed Cyfa. Susan did enjoy the Church youth club on a Wednesday evening. Her mother in her own interview said, 'she probably told you I make her go but she wouldn't do anything unless kicked'.

The obvious difference between her and the older boy and girl was that she was adopted and, unlike her adopted parents, was of mixed race in an area where there were few black people. Her mother was aware of the difficulties she will face and hoped 'she doesn't get too battered as a coloured youngster in a white society'. Her mother was unusual in insisting on attendance at Church/Sunday school and Susan seemed to reject the 'boring' practice of Christianity rather than the beliefs. She spoke more favourably of Church 'where my nan lives the Vicar doesn't do a sermon and the service is only half an hour'. Her opposition may have been simply a rebellion against her mother, she rarely had to listen to the sermon anyway as she was in Pathfinders, and an assertion of what she saw as her right to make up her own mind. In the same way she disliked the Bible story based RE at her church primary school where 'they kept drilling [Bible stories] into our minds', but found the broader RE at secondary school 'more interesting'. Asked why people go to church, she said;

> Most of them are committed Christians ... like those at Living Waters [a charismatic group at her church]. They like to do it.

After GCSE Susan went to a sixth form college twenty miles away rather than stay at Penvollard school sixth form to take A levels. One of her best GCSE grades was in Religious Education. She still went to the Anglican Church and was 'not very keen' but also went to Cyfa and enjoyed it.

Case 2   A mother brought up as a Catholic and her family

John and Pauline are twins who were living with both their parents in a small village of about 100 people. It is interesting to look at their differing attitudes to religion because their home, school and cultural influences are the same, other than differences due to gender. At the first interview they attended the village aided school, described in chapter 5, where their mother had just been appointed as a parent governor. The family moved down to the area because their mother thought the children 'could get on better' and was pleased that the school was a Church school and small.

Their mother worked part-time as a district nurse and their father was manager of a plant hire firm. Their mother was brought up as a Roman Catholic and went to Church with her family. She went to convent school and 'rattled through confirmation at ten ... I fiddled with my veil most of the time'. Her children were baptised and had first communion. She would like the children to be confirmed 'when they want to be, from commitment' but her husband 'feels that socially they should be confirmed because it is less difficult when they are older', meaning it would be less difficult for them to go to Church later on if they were already confirmed. She felt that 'Confirmation is a big sacrament and it should mean something for them, not just the long white dress'. She continued going to Church in her twenties 'but it didn't mean anything to me'. Once she was married and 'a mum' in her thirties, she was baptised in the Baptist Church by full immersion 'it meant a hell of a lot to me'. Her son recalled the Baptist Church as being 'brilliant fun' and at separate interviews both children mentioned the same Bible story as their favourite and said they had heard it first at that Church.

In 1984, when the twins were nine years old, the family moved down to the south west because their mother felt it would be a better place to bring up the children. They lived in temporary accommodation and could go to the local Baptist Church. However once settled in the village the nearest

Baptist Church was over ten miles away. At the first interview the mother was going to the Catholic Church in Penvollard and the twins, in the last year of primary school, were coming with her about twice a month. She was also on the Parochial Church Council of the Anglican Church in her village and was trying to get a young people's service going. The Sunday school had closed before the interview. She was concerned that her children were not keen on going to Church and was trying various churches in the area to find one she and they liked. She saw it as her responsibility to 'give guidelines' to the children and 'sow the seed' even though it is 'up to them to choose which way they go after'.

By the second interview she was going to another village to the Church of England because her daughter liked to serve there. John and his brother, one year older, were by then only going 'when made to on high days and holidays' ... 'not as much as [mother] would like'. She felt that her husband, as a non-believer, undermined what she was trying to achieve.

She was planning to try another village Church because there had been a change of Vicar at the church where Pauline served and the new one was a non-stipendary minister who had 'no rapport with the kids'. John said he enjoyed going to Church at Christmas and Easter but 'the Vicar makes the sermon boring'. Joanna enjoys serving but thinks 'some of the hymns are quite dreary'.

At the age of ten both children were 'at a bit of a stage' according to their mother and while she encouraged them to come to Church she felt she could not force them 'or they will dig their heels in'. By the age of twelve John was going less often and she 'used bribery' to get him to go at all, whereas Pauline was going more regularly as she enjoyed serving. John no longer read the Bible except in RE lessons at school but Pauline still read it at home. Both stressed the sermon when asked what the Vicar/priest does . Pauline said 'he just says a long speech in the middle of it, not sure otherwise' and John, 'he just gives sermons'. Both agreed that there is a 'benevolent power or God behind the universe', though John said later that although there 'probably is a God' he had 'not thought about it'. Pauline did sometimes think about what God might be like, 'people say when you go to heaven your soul goes up. I just think about a round object'. She was more positive about religion in school than her brother She agreed that 'it is important that children learn about Christianity as part of our heritage', while he disagreed; she agreed that RE is an important part of education, while he had no particular opinion and she agreed that 'other religions' should be taught in school, while he disagreed and said 'not many are interested in it'.

The twins mother wanted them to have a religious upbringing but not the same background as she herself had with a Roman Catholic family and convent school. She said 'we were the last generation brought up when the Church was rigid, I am 40 ... I went twice a day ... life was very influenced by church activities ... almost too much, it became oppressive'. She remembered a priest once telling her that 'your first allegiance is to God, your next is to the family and then to the Church'. She is 'a bit more liberal now' and 'will sometimes give in and put the family first, because you can give allegiance to God from home'. Asked if she would call herself religious, she said;

> I suppose I am. Christmas and Easter mean a great deal in this house, aside from the presents and chocolate Easter eggs. I wonder if it will be the same for the children though.

Her husband went on special festivals but 'goes for me ... [he] makes it clear it doesn't mean anything to him and [the children] are heavily influenced by their father. He makes comments sometimes ... not helpful'. She 'hopes something will rub off' on the children. She was fairly optimistic about the future because although 'in the sixties we got out' of the Church along with other institutions 'there is a gradual curve back'. She went to 'young gatherings like Bible rallies 'taking a day off work when they are held nearby and found;

> The young are practical Christians ... practically caring for each other, they may not be in church, come from house groups and so on.

She thinks 'there will be a livelier more practical form of religion'.

The future, in her opinion, lay with non-institutional Christians, while Churches like her own village Church were, she thought, 'dead'. She had 'a need for a Church ... to attend a building with other people' though 'not saying I need a set format'. She considered herself fortunate that her profession allows her to show she was a Christian by wearing a cross with her uniform so that her patients would talk about religion if they wanted to. Although the twins had the same home background, Pauline conformed more in terms of religious attitudes and for longer in religious practice. It might be expected that their father's attitudes would affect John more strongly, as he grew up in a household where religion was important to his mother but not to his father or older brother. His mother saw him as more headstrong and rebellious than his sister and worried that 'he might get in with the wrong crowd.' She thought Pauline 'will make a good wife and mum' but did not expect 'anything marvellous' in terms of academic achievement.

By age 16 John was doing 'A' levels and Pauline a Family and Community care course. Pauline hoped to train as a nurse and John to go into the RAF. By then they had both 'dropped out' and had not been to a church for a few years but their mother still attended.

Case 3 A Jehovah's Witness family

Paul came from a Jehovah's Witness family and was the only boy, out of the 22 interviewed in the three schools, who attended a religious service every week. His father was a self-employed builder and his mother was at home with a younger child, but previously worked part-time in a shop. The family lived in a modern council house near Penvollard Church school. He attended Penvollard County Junior school rather than the Church of England school. Religion was 'very very important' to both parents 'it's a way of life'. Both parents and the four children were present during the interviews. The mother was brought up as a Witness from the age of six and baptised at age 14. Her mother was Methodist before that and her father nominally Church of England. Paul's father became a Witness as a teenager. His mother, Paul's grandmother, started going to meetings but then stopped. He carried on and was baptised at 16. His mother has now moved down to the area where they live and is baptised herself. Paul's parents were clearly used to talking about their faith and anticipating the obvious questions asked by outsiders, for example why they do not celebrate Christmas. At the County school Paul said most of his friends were Jehovah's witnesses, there were five in the school at that time. At the comprehensive school there were six in the lower school. He did not take part in religious education, assemblies or religious plays at the County Junior school.

Paul's social life was filled by his religious activities throughout his childhood. The whole family went to meetings at Kingdom Hall twice a week and had a meeting in their own house once a week. Most of these activities were for the whole family together but there had been separate social activities for the older children. His parents aimed to do ten hours visiting a month and Paul had been out with his mother on the morning of the first interview, when he was ten. Paul's mother disagreed strongly with the statement 'religion is something children have to make up their own minds about' saying 'parents have an obligation and duty to teach their children religion. They will come to a decision when they feel ready, around their early teens'. He was the only child out of the 38 to read the Bible regularly, reading it at home and at Kingdom Hall.

The interest his parents had in education differed from the usual view of parental interest as interest in academic success, the child reaching his or her potential and having a good career or job. As Witnesses his parents did not expect the world as it is to last much longer. Asked about her hopes for her son's future and what she hoped he would gain from his education his mother said;

> The system will be brought to an end by God anyway. 'The time will come when he will have the opportunity to live for ever and

never grow old or ill. My hope is for him to live for ever in a perfect paradise. As long as he stays on until 16 or 17 ... not at all interested in university.

At the first interview she said she would like him to grow up to do missionary work full-time.

Before he went to Penvollard comprehensive school her worries were about 'the rubbish they teach up there. Evolution taught as fact not theory, mythology taught '..and she also disliked the 'emphasis on social work and fund raising' feeling that 'pressure is put on children ..they are not given enough freedom to express themselves'. She gave as an example the 'non-uniform' day when children paid not to wear uniform. There was pressure to join in but her elder son did not. She had also heard that 'some teachers detest Witnesses and pick on the children' and had 'heard of them withholding meal tickets'. However, once Paul had started second year she had not encountered any problems with the teachers. She would want Paul to remain to some extent detached from school activities, not going to assemblies or RE and not taking part in after school activities which might interfere with his religion.

For Paul the clash between values of home and school is anticipated as his is an embattled religion which rejects this world. He saw himself as a Witness answering questions on his beliefs with 'we' rather than 'I' and repeating learned phrases. In answer to the question 'why do people go to a Church?' he replied 'to learn true and survive through Armageddon'. His learning was more structured than any of the non-Witness children. He attended meetings more often and had preparatory work to do for them. Although his mother said she felt children are not given enough freedom for self expression at school, it would seem to be difficult for Paul to decide not to follow his parents' beliefs until he is independent because such a decision would cut him off from the central focus of family life. His day to day activities are reminiscent of the descriptions given by older members of their Christian upbringing. The leader of the Methodist Sunday school near the Village Church school started teaching there in the 1930s. He recalled his boyhood when chapel activities filled a large part of his free time. 'On Sunday I would go to chapel at 11, Sunday school at 2.30, milk the cows and go to chapel in the evening, and it was supposed to be a day of rest. There would be young folk's meetings at [Penvollard] and at the manse.' For a modern child in the same village there was only one service with Sunday school.

By age sixteen Paul was still at school doing an A level in textiles and GCSE dance. He had been in school productions and enjoyed dance. He was still a Witness but not yet baptised. His parents appeared to have made some compromises, for example by letting Paul take part in a school play and dancing. His father said 'you have to allow a balance'.

His mother was contacted again when Paul was twenty, in 1996. He had moved into his own flat locally, which was owned by a Witness family. He was working in a wine merchants. Paul still attended Kingdom Hall and was involved in the preaching work. His friends were Witnesses. His elder brother had moved away, was active in the congregation where he lived and had a girlfriend who was a Witness. One child had stopped attending and was living away from home. The mother said those who had been disfellowshipped can return to the faith and a woman had recently been readmitted. She and her husband had insisted that if one of the children dropped out of the Witnesses they could no longer live at home but felt that 'strong arm tactics do not work'.

Case 4 - A 'born again' Christian mother and her family

Stephen lived in the outskirts of the market town in a terraced cottage. His mother was a hairdresser but had not worked since he was born. He had a brother two years younger than himself. His father worked in a timber mill. Stephen's mother was brought up as a Methodist and went with her mother and grandfather to the local chapel about 20 miles from Penvollard. She stopped going when she grew up and Stephen was not baptised. When he was a baby she took him to 'tiny tots' at the Anglican Church with a group of mothers who had had babies at the same time. They were going on to the Church school and she wanted him to have a 'spiritual side' to his education although she was not a Christian at that time. She described her conversion to Christianity in 1983, when Stephen was eight;

> I am a born again Christian ... I had always believed in God and that Jesus died but the knowledge was in my head not in my heart. I met some people on a beach and they thought I was a Christian. Someone else said 'Why do you send your child to a Church school when you are not a Christian?' ... little things added up and made me think.

She started going to the Methodist Church because she had been a Methodist and by the first interview said, 'Christianity is everything to me, my life'. She read the Bible everyday and belonged to a Christian drama group attached to the Methodist Church. She also went to a charismatic group which met at the Anglican Church. Her dream would be that her son 'would be called to be a Vicar' and she prayed for Christian wives for her sons.

At the first interview when Stephen was in the last year at the Church town school, he went to Sunday school with his younger brother at the Methodist Chapel attended by his mother. He was enthusiastic about Sunday school saying he enjoyed going but said he might go to the

Anglican Pathfinders when he was eleven. He was also enthusiastic about school RE saying 'I like it. We learn about things, there could be more of it. The rest of the class don't agree with me.' The latter statement was borne out by the fact that only one other child was positive about religious education of the eighteen children interviewed from his class. He was one of the few to give a religious reason for having assemblies saying 'we have them to help us when we grow up to become Christians'. He owned a Bible which he had bought himself and read it 'sometimes'. Asked if he noticed any differences between his school and other schools he knew he said 'others are not Christian schools, Church schools'. He gave clear full answers to questions on the life of Jesus and knew 3/4 of the Old Testament stories. His mother said she had insisted the boys came to Church with her when she became a Christian, although they did not want to go but now they go voluntarily. She described her husband as a 'non-believer' and said 'I can't force them [to go to Church] because they can go and ask their father and he will say they don't have to go'. Though it is important to her that they go to Church or Sunday school 'you can't force them'. Whether Stephen was confirmed would be 'a decision he would have to make, nothing to do with me'.

At the second interview Stephen was at the comprehensive school, in the second year, aged twelve. He no longer went to chapel, no longer had a Bible and dissociated himself from Christians in his answers. Asked if he ever thought about God he said;

> A long time ago someone might have made it up. You can't prove it. The Bible could just have been written. Sometimes I think about what he is like but life's a bit too short, get on with it ... have the best you can.

Asked why he thought people go to Church he said;

> because they are a Christian or want to make themselves look honourable or high or good ... make other people look up to them. In the olden days you said 'I go to Church' and think 'he must be a good man'. Nowadays people still look up a bit. I bet the Queen goes to Church every Sunday and she's looked up to isn't she? ... [In Church] they sing to *their* God and Jesus.

He described the Vicar or minister as 'a leader, someone special' and, perhaps thinking of himself, added, ' ... but everyone should have their say ... if they disagree they should be able to say so'.

He had stopped going to Sunday school because he 'got fed up with it' and 'got cross with mum going on about it'. He 'disagreed strongly' with the ideas that it is important to go to Church or Sunday school and disagreed with the view that RE is an important part of education. However, he 'agreed strongly' that RE teaches about right and wrong and agreed that he should learn about Christianity as part of his heritage. He had no particular hobbies at the first interview. At the second his mother said he wanted to join the army cadets when he is thirteen and had camouflage trousers and jacket for Christmas. He said he played a lot in the woods building camps and went to athletics at school in the season.

His mother felt that his peer group had something to do with his attitude to religion.

> At the senior school they are called 'Jesus creeps' if they do anything religious. They have to be tough to stand up to that.

His younger brother, at the age Stephen was at the first interview, still went to the Methodist Sunday school. However he dropped out at age thirteen. Stephen stayed at school to do maths, art and textiles at 'A' level. He never attended church but his mother still had hope that he would come back to it and reported that 'he has a Christian friend so is asking questions'. In 1996 she was going to the Christian group led by a former Methodist minister who had had to leave the Methodist Church because he disagreed with their position on homosexuality and non-Christian faiths. Her husband had been attending with her for about one year and although he had not made a commitment, had said it must be affecting him. Stephen was working locally and living at home.

Appendix 2
Methodology

A particular town was selected for a case study in order to examine the religiosity of a group of families with young children and their community. The community, a small town in the south west of England here called Penvollard, was a convenient size to study and had only two schools for junior age children, an aided school and a county school. It had the particular religious characteristics of parts of the south west; a strong Methodist tradition, a low proportion of Catholics and few representatives of `other' faiths. The only religious presence in Penvollard was Christian and there were no Catholic schools in the town or surrounding area, nor any church secondary schools . Thus the Church of England influence might be clearer in Penvollard than it would have been in a multi-faith area with a choice of denominational schools at primary and secondary level. Most of the existing empirical research interprets 'religiosity' and 'religious attitudes' as 'Christian religiosity' and 'attitudes towards Christianity' and so is more relevant to the chosen town than it would be to many urban areas of Britain.

The study 'followed' children and their families from their final year in primary education to the end of compulsory schooling. Families were contacted when the children were 10/11 (referred to as the first interview) in 1985-86, two years later in 1987-88 when they were aged 12/13 (second interview) and again by telephone or letter when they were 16/17 in March 1992. The third school included in the case study was a small, rural school outside Penvollard, which, although it had aided status, served as the only school for the surrounding area. Out of the three school only Penvollard Church school was oversubscribed. Thus the mothers in the sample represented a group who had positively opted for a church school, another group whose children went to the county school instead and a third group whose local school happened to be a church school. Most children from all three groups would be attending Penvollard comprehensive school by the second interview. The nearest Catholic aided primary school to Penvollard was about 18 miles away and a further group of seven families, both Catholic and non-Catholic, were interviewed and followed up in the same way in a subsidiary study used to focus on comparisons with the Church of England aided schools. The schools themselves were studied through interviews with headteachers, teachers and governors and through curriculum statements and school handbooks.

Contact with the families was made as follows. All the children in their final year of primary education were given letters from the school to their parents requesting interviews in their own homes with the child and his or her mother.[1] The overall response rate was 50 per cent in both the Church schools and 38 per cent in the county junior school. The final number of families involved was 38 (excluding the seven families from the Catholic school) of whom 37 were followed through to age 16/17, one family having moved just after the first interview. Judging by the addresses of those who did respond they were representative of the schools' intakes in terms of social class and, judging by churchgoing and baptism rates the sample was only slightly skewed in favour of practising Christian families. 13 per cent of the mothers were regular churchgoers (not necessarily every week), a similar figure to national surveys. The English Church census gives a figure of 10 per cent attendance in Cornwall on one specific Sunday (Brierley 1991). With this small sample no claims can be made about the generalisability of the findings but parallels are drawn with other research.

Measuring the religiosity of mothers and children

The purpose of the case-study was to build up a picture of the context within which the child's religious beliefs and attitudes were being formed, as well as to measure those beliefs and attitudes and the way in which they changed. Longitudinal studies have been carried out elsewhere using attitude scales but, as already mentioned, these were administered to successive years in the same schools rather than to identifiable children, and, details of changes in family life or other circumstances were not available (Francis 1992).

The social factors affecting a child's religiosity were assumed to be the home and family, the school, local churches and the community within which the child lived. A study of the economy, recreation and religious organizations of the community provided the background to the study of schools and individual families. Information came from official statistics including Census data and figures collected by the churches and key informants including governors, teachers, clergy and church members as presented in chapters 5 and 6. This information provided the background to the in-depth interviews with mothers and children.

The interviews were based on questionnaires. The mothers' questionnaires for both interviews were kept as similar as possible to allow comparison between answers, although the specific questions on the child's current school required different wording. For children the main difference in the questionnaires was that questions on religious knowledge asked in the first interview, were replaced in the second by the attitude statements used with the mothers.

Mothers' questionnaire

Section A (Interview 1 questions A1-A6, interview 2 questions A1-A3). In the first interview this section explored reasons for the child attending a particular primary school, the admission procedures and what differences, if any, mothers saw between local primary schools. Additional questions for mothers with children at a church aided school asked whether they were aware the school was a church school before they chose it and if they had any particular expectations of such schools. These questions were intended to explore some of the points made in chapter 4 on the role of church schools, i.e. they are popular with parents but not necessarily for 'religious' reasons; parents expect church schools to offer traditional education, church schools should have strong ties with the local community and offer 'good' religious education and worship.

At the second interview mothers were asked about differences between their child's primary and secondary schools; their contact with the school and how their child had settled down there. This gave mothers an opportunity to reflect on their child's primary school and compare their expectations of secondary school with the reality.

Section B (Interview 1 questions B1-B8 interview 2 questions B1-B4) Children have a variety of activities available inside and outside school and in the second section mothers were asked about their child's activities and interests. This was to discover the range of activities available, the part still played by religious organizations and any changes in this respect as the child moved on to secondary school. This was followed by question B2 which talked the mother through the child's religious life history. Mothers were then asked whether their children mentioned assemblies, religious education, local clergy visits to school or religious plays (question B3). and the degree of involvement they had in their child's school, including visits for assemblies or to Church services (question B4). This was to assess the mothers' knowledge and interest in their child's schooling and any changes when the child moved from primary to secondary school. The additional four questions in the first interview were about the choice of secondary school to which the child would soon be transferring. Mothers were asked about any differences between the child's primary school and the chosen

143

secondary school, any worries about the transition and whether they had visited the school yet.

Section C (Both interviews questions C1-C11) The first question asked about other children in the family and mothers gave information on their age, school or occupation without further questions. In the second interview the information was brought up to date. Mothers were then talked through their own religious life history and that of their husbands and other children. In the second interview changes in practice could be monitored and any gaps filled in. As well as recording such changes, mothers were asked why they thought these changes had occurred. Question C3 was an apparently simple question; 'would you call yourself religious?' followed by asking 'what do you mean by religious?'. This brought out the mothers' views on religion and religious people before the more specific attitude questions (C5-C7). Mothers were then asked about Bible ownership and reading to compare with more public aspects of religiosity and their children's answers.

Having established the family religiosity in terms of participation in organized religion, the interview moved on to attitudes and beliefs. The next question, C5 asked them to rate the importance of religion in their lives on a four point rating scale (very important, fairly important, not very important, not important). Then a list of different aspects of religion were read out and they were asked to say how important or unimportant they thought each one was on the same scale. More people believe than attend public worship and, in Britain some public figures still make a clear link between morality and religion, as discussed in chapter 3. Mothers might therefore be reluctant to say religion was not at all important to them, lest they be seen to be uncaring or immoral. They might rate the public aspects of religion (worship and missionary work) as less important than the moral aspects (giving to others and leading a good life) but leave the private aspect (personal prayer) up to the individual. Mothers made comments as they answered which explained the reasons for their ratings and why they considered themselves religious or not religious. Thus it became clear why a mother who did not attend a church called herself religious, when she rated 'going to a place of worship' as an unimportant part of religion, but 'giving to others' as very important and something which could not be done while sitting in a church.

There followed a series of attitude statements about religion and religious education (question C7). Mothers were asked to choose from a five point scale with the options; 'agree strongly', 'agree', 'no particular opinion', 'disagree' or 'disagree strongly'. At the second interview they were asked whether they thought their ideas had changed and if there were any particular reasons for the differences. If the mothers rarely thought about religion and religious education the answers might simply be given at random and changes not be significant.

To add to the picture being built up of the mother's views on schools and religion the next question, C8, was about her hopes for her child's future and what he or she might gain from education. These answers could be related to other variables; for example the child's age, gender or social class. The final questions on occupations provided a measure of social class (question C9-C10). The type of house and location was noted as a further indication of economic position.

Children's' questionnaire

Section A (questions A1-A7) Children were asked about their favourite subjects at school and then in more detail about religious education and assemblies, focussing on what they were learning about religion at the time of the interview and on recent assemblies (questions A1-A6). The section finished by asking whether they had thought about why they had school assemblies.

Section B Children were asked about hobbies and interests and their current and past church attendance (question B1-B2). Changes in their involvement in church or chapel activities and in their attitudes to them, could be monitored as they moved from childhood to adolescence. At the second interview questions were asked next on Bible ownership, reading, whether the child had a favourite Bible story and, if so, where they had heard it. However in the first interview these questions were put in the next section as a precursor to the questions on Bible knowledge.

It seemed likely that the influence of a church primary school might be more significant if children drew their friends from those who attended the church school with them and continued these friendships into secondary school. Children were therefore asked about the schools their friends attended and, at the first interview, were also asked if they were aware of any differences between their school and other schools (interview 1 question B3).

Section C The final section consisted of completely different questions in the first and second interviews. When they were 10/11 the children were asked questions on the Bible, as explained under section B, and then asked about some Old Testament characters and the life of Jesus as a test of basic knowledge of Christianity which could be compared with the school they attended, its syllabus for religious education and church attendance. At the second interview children were asked for their opinion on the same series of attitude statements used with mothers (question C7) so that their answers could be compared. It was found in the pilot study that children of 10/11

145

tended not to have any opinion on the statements so they were not used in the first interview. The second interview ended with four open questions to try to find out more about their ideas of the church and the language they would use to describe God. The children were asked, 'Do you think there is a God?'. The follow up question was 'What do you think God is?' or 'What made you decide there is no God?'. They were then asked why they thought people went to church, what people do in church and what the Vicar does.

The questionnaire was originally devised as a structured questionnaire with a mixture of open and closed questions. The choices made from a rating scale and replies to closed questions provided a picture of the family's religiosity and more general values and attitudes. However the comments made and recorded as the interviews progressed told how the mothers made sense of their replies. They made sense, to themselves and to me, through the describing of people and incidents in their lives which had influenced them. In the second interview when they knew what sort of questions would be asked and were more relaxed, the 'stories' became fuller and religious experiences, family crises and childhood experiences were described. These 'stories' provided one way of understanding and explaining the patterns of responses. The children also told 'stories' when answering the questions which referred to things they had experienced, like religious education and assemblies. Perhaps because they had at 10-13 years old had fewer experiences relevant to the issues and were less relaxed talking to an unknown adult, the children made fewer comments and more often had no particular opinion.

The set questions allowed comparisons to be made between mothers and children from different schools and to measure changes over time but the recording of the interviewees thoughts and comments as they answered provided richer qualitative data.

Notes

1. It was expected that children would be likely to live with their natural mother and that the mother would have most responsibility for the child at 10/11 years old. At the first interview all the children were living with their natural mothers but six were not living with their natural fathers and two of these had no contact with him. Three of the children had step-fathers.

146

Appendix 3
Interview schedules

INTERVIEW WITH MOTHER OF CHILD IN YEAR 6 (age 10/11)

Section A

A1 Did you consider any other schools in the area before you decided to send (child) to (school)?

A2 What made you choose (school) first/in the end?

A3 Do you see any differences between (child's school) and other primary schools in the area?

(note details)

A4 How old was (child) when you decided to send him/her to (school)?

Did you have to put his/her name on a waiting list?

Did you visit the school?

[CHURCH SCHOOL MOTHERS ONLY]

A5 Did you know that (school) was a church school before you chose it?

A6 What do you see as the purpose of the Church of England's involvement in primary education today?

Section B

Next I would like to ask you some questions about (child's) interests.

B1 Does [child] have any regular activities or belong to any clubs or organisations

       a) in school? (list)
       b) out of school ? (list)

B2 (If not mentioned) Does [child] ever go to Church/Sunday school ?
(if [child] ever goes cover these points)
Where does [child] go?
How regularly does [child] go?
Service or Sunday school?
Does [child] go with anyone or on his/her own??
Does [child] enjoy going ?
Do you encourage [child] to go?

(if pattern of Church-going has changed)
When did [child] stop going or start going ?
Was there any particular reason why [child] stopped going or started going?
Is [child] baptised/christened ?
(if appropriate) Is [child] confirmed or do you expect [child] to be confirmed?

B3 Going back to school now: Does he/she ever mention
          a)   assemblies
          b)   religious education
          c)   the local Vicar coming into school
          d)   religious plays
          e)   concerts/Church going with the school.
(note any details)

B4 Are you able to attend assemblies or church services connected with the school?

B5 Looking on to when [child] leaves [school] do you expect him/her to go on to the comprehensive?
(If no: Do you have another school in mind for him/her?)

B6 Do you have any worries about [child] moving on to [school]?
(note any comments)

148

B7 Thinking of the differences between [child's school] and the secondary school, would you expect there to be any important differences?

Note differences:
in the way religion is taught
in assemblies
standards of discipline
type of teachers
social differences
others.

B8 Have you visited the school yet?

Section C

I would like to ask some questions about yourself and the rest of the family.

C1 Do you have any other children ?
(note sex, ages, school/college/work)

C2 Do you attend church /chapel?

If yes: denomination
How often do you go?
Which service do you go to (time and type)?
Have you always gone to (denomination) ? (talk through religious life history)
Did you go as a child? with family?
Did you go to a church school?
Were you baptised?
Were you confirmed?
When did you stop going etc.

If pattern of church-going has changed from last time
When did you stop going/start going (etc) ?
Was there any particular reason why you stopped going/started going?

C3 Would you call yourself religious? (probe for definition)

C4 Do you have a Bible in your home?
Do you ever read it ?
(How do you come to have a Bible?)

Next I would like to ask you for your opinion on some issues to do with religion and religious education.

(Give printed card with choices:)
>   Very important
>   Fairly important
>   Not very important
>   Not important)

Please choose the one nearest to what you think and make any comments you like as we go along.

C5 How important is religion in your life?

C6 What do you think are the most important aspects of religion? (I will read out some aspects of religion; ould you say how important or unimportant each is).

a) Going to a place of worship
b) Believing in God
c) Personal prayer
d) Leading a good life
e) Giving to others
f) Being an active missionary in your community

If you turn the card over you will see some more attitudes:
>   Agree strongly
>   Agree
>   No particular opinion
>   Disagree
>   Disagree strongly

Could you choose the attitude nearest to your own on the statements I will read out,and make any comments you like as we go through them.

C7 There are some mysteries in life that science will never explain.

There is a benevolent power behind the universe (substitute 'good' if necessary)

The Churches have little influence or importance these days.

Religion is something which children have to make up their own minds about.

Religious education teaches children about right and wrong.

Children ought to know about Christianity as part of our heritage.

It is important for children to go to Church or Sunday school.

It is important for children to attend a religious assembly everyday at school.

Children should be taught about different religions at school.

Religious education is an important part of childrens' education.
(Take back card)

C8 Could you tell me what sort of hopes you have for (child's) future?
    What do you hope [child] will gain from his/her education ?

C9 Finally could you tell me if you have any paid employment?
    (job,full/part time) Do you work locally?

C10 Is you husband employed ? (job?) Does he work locally ?
    No: unemployed/disabled/retired?

I would like to talk to you again in a couple of years time when [child] is at secondary school. Would you mind if I contacted you again then?
(Note type of housing)

INTERVIEW WITH CHILD IN YEAR 6 (AGE 10/11)

Name:
Date of birth:
School:

Section A

First of all I would like you to tell me about some of the things you do at school.

A1 What subjects do you like best at school?

A2 What do you like most about (name of subject/s)?

A3 You learn about religion in school (about the Bible, God, Jesus) have you done anything like that recently that you can remember?

A4 Do you find it interesting or not? (record attitude)

A5 You have assemblies at school -have you taken part in an assembly ? (what did you do last time you took part?)

A6 What did you do in assembly today (on Friday for weekend). Can you remember?

A7 Have you ever thought about why you have assemblies in school?

Section B

Next I would like to talk to you about your hobbies and interests.

B1 Do you belong to any clubs or organisations
        a) in school? (list)
        b) out of school ? (list)

B2 Do you go to Church or Sunday school ?
    Yes: [cover these topics)
    Which Church do you go to?
    How often do you go?
    Who do you usually go with ?
    Do you go to Sunday school/junior church ?

Do you enjoy going to Church/Sunday school (what do you like/dislike about it?)
Do you ever take part in the service in Church? (what do you do?)
Are there any other activities for children your age at Church (what are they?).
[if appropriate] Are you confirmed./do you expect to be confirmed later on?

No : Have you ever gone?
Was there any particular reason why you stopped going?
Does anyone else in the family go now?

B3 Do you have friends who go to other schools?
(if yes) Have you noticed any ways their schools are different from your school?
(if yes) In what ways are they different?
B4 Thinking of friends you go around with, are most of them from your school or from other schools?

B5 How did you meet your friends from other schools?

Section C

Lastly I would like to talk about religion and the Bible.
C1 Do you know if there is a Bible in the houe?
Do you have one of your own?
(if yes) Can you remember who gave it to you?
Do you know what sort of Bible it is?

C2 Do you ever read the Bible?
Where do you read it? (school, SS, homework etc..)

C3 Do you have a favourite story from the Bible?
(note what it is)

C4 (if yes) Can you remember where you heard that story?

C5 I am going to read the names of some people who have stories about them in the Bible. I would like you to tell me if you remember hearing any of these stories.

Adam and Eve ... Do you remember a story about them? (If yes..ask if they can tell you anything about them and note details)

Moses ... Do you remember any stories about him? (any details?)

Abraham and Issac ... Do you remember anything about them?

David and Goliath ... Do you remember a story about them?

C6 In the New Testament in the Bible there are lots of stories about Jesus. Who was Jesus?

C7 Do you know where people say he was born?

C8 When do people remember Jesus's birth?
Have you ever been in a nativity play or other religious play? (where/what were you)

C9 When do Christians remember Jesus's death and rising from the dead? (suitable comment- you know a lot about the Bible etc)

Finally I would like to talk about the secondary school you are going to:

C9 Are you going to [local comprehensive]? (if no: which school are you going to?)

C10 Do you have a brother or sister at the school?

C11 In what ways do you think it will be different from [present school]? How do you feel about going there?

INTERVIEW WITH MOTHER OF CHILD IN YEAR 8 (age 12/13)

Section A

A1 Last time I saw you (child) was soon to go to [secondary school]and we talked about the differences you expected to find between the two schools. Was it as you expected? Any particular differences compared with primary/junior school?

[Note differences in the way religion is taught
    in assemblies
    standards of discipline
    type of teacher
    social differences
    any others?]

A2 Have you visited the school- how often do you go ?
Are you more or less involved than you were in (name of primary school)? Why is this?

A3 How did (child) settle in at the new school?

Section B

Next I would like to ask you some questions about [child's] interests.

B1 Does [child] have any regular activities or belong to any clubs or organisations
    a) in school? (list)
    b) out of school ? (list)

B2 (If not mentioned) Does [child] ever go to Church/Sunday school ?
(if [child] ever goes cover these points)
Where does [child] go?
How regularly does [child] go?
Service or Sunday school?
Does [child] go with anyone or on his/her own?
Does [child] enjoy going ?
Do you encourage [child] to go?

(if pattern of Church-going has changed from last time)
When did [child] stop going or start going ?

Was there any particular reason why [child] stopped going or started going?
Is [child] baptised/christened ?
(if appropriate) Is [child] confirmed or do you expect [child] to be confirmed?

B3 Going back to school now: Does [child] ever mention:
      a) assemblies
      b) religious education
      c) the local Vicar coming into school
      d) religious plays/concerts/church going with the school.(note any details)

Section C

I would like to ask some questions about yourself and the rest of the family. Have you always lived in this area? (if not when did you move /where from/is husband local?)

C1 (If appropriate) What are your other children doing now ?

C2 Do you attend church /chapel?

    If yes: denomination
    How often do you go?
    Which service do you go to (time and type)?
    Have you always gone to [denomination]? (talk through religious life history, filling in gaps from last interview)
    Did you go as a child? with family?
    Did you go to a church school?
    Were you baptised? Were you confirmed?
    When did you stop going etc.

If pattern of church-going has changed from last time
When did you stop going/start going (etc) ?
Was there any particular reason why you stopped going/started going?

(Questions C3-C7 were asked in the last interview-the respondant will be asked to comment on differences)
C3 Would you call yourself religious? (probe for definition)

C4 Do you have a Bible in your home?
    Do you ever read it ?
    (How do you come to have a Bible?)

156

Next I would like to ask you for your opinion on some issues to do with religion and religious education.

(Give card)
Very important
Fairly important
Not very important
Not important)

Please choose the one nearest to what you think and make any comments you like as we go along.

C5 How important is religion in your life?

C6 What do you think are the most important aspects of religion? (I will read out some aspects of religion;could you say how important or unimportant each is).

   a) Going to a place of worship
   b) Believing in God
   c) Personal prayer
   d) Leading a good life
   e) Giving to others
   f) Being an active missionary in your community

If you turn the card over you will see some more attitudes:
Agree strongly
Agree
No particular opinion
Disagree
Disagree strongly

Could you choose the attitude nearest to your own on the statements I will read out,and make any comments you like as we go through them.

C7 There are some mysteries in life that science will never explain.

There is a benevolent power behind the universe (substitute 'good' if
· necessary)

The Churches have little influence or importance these days.

Religion is something which children have to make up their own minds about.

157

Religious education teaches children about right and wrong.

Children ought to know about Christianity as part of our heritage.

It is important for children to go to Church or Sunday school.

It is important for children to attend religious assemblies at school.

Children should be taught about different religions at school.

Religious education is an important part of childrens' education.
(Take back card)

Do you think your ideas have changed from the last time I saw you ?
(try to find out if there are particular reasons for any differences-or
does the respondant just give an answer because asked for it. Are these
attitudes she thinks about or not?).

C8 Could you tell me what sort of hopes you have for [child's] future?
What do you hope [child] will gain from his/her education ?

C9 Finally could you tell me if you have any paid employment?
(job,full/part time) Do you work locally?

C10 Is your husband employed ? (job?) Does he work locally ?
No: unemployed/disabled/retired?

Thank you for letting me talk to you again and see (child).

(Note type of housing)

INTERVIEW WITH CHILD IN SECONDARY SCHOOL YEAR 8 (AGE 12/13)

Name:
Date of birth:
School:

Section A

First of all I would like you to tell me about some of the things you do at school.

A1 What subjects do you like best at school?

A2 What do you like most about (name of subject/s)?

A3 You have religious education at school -what have you been doing in RE recently?

A4 Do you find it interesting or not? (record attitude)
    You learnt about religion at (name of primary/junior school) too- do you find it more or less interesting now? (note any differences remarked on)

A5 You have assemblies at school -have you taken part in an assembly ? (what did you do last time you took part?)

A6 What did you do in assembly today (on Friday for weekend),can you remember?

A7 Have you ever thought about why you have assemblies in school?

Section B

Next I would like to talk to you about your hobbies and interests.

B1 Do you belong to any clubs or organisations
        a) in school? (list)
        b) out of school ? (list)

B2 Do you go to Church or Sunday school ?

Yes: [cover these topics)
Which Church do you go to?
How often do you go?
Who do you usually go with ?
Do you go to Sunday school/junior church ?
Do you enjoy going to Church/Sunday school (what do you like/dislike about it?)
Do you ever take part in the service in Church? (what do you do?)
Are there any other activities for children your age at Church (what are they?).
[if appropriate] Are you confirmed ... do you expect to be confirmed later on?

No: Have you ever gone? (check last interview).
Was there any particular reason why you stopped going?
Does anyone else in the family go now?

B3 Do you have a Bible of your own?
Who gave it to you?
Do you know what sort it is?

B4 Do you ever read the Bible (if yes-where do you read it?)

B5 Do you have a favourite story from the Bible? (name)

B6 Can you remember where you first heard that story?

B7 Thinking of friends you go around with, were most of them at the same primary school as you ?

B8 Do you go round with them out of school as well ? (have you got other friends you meet outside school?)

Section C

In these last questions I want to know your own opinion, so there are not any right answers-I just want to know what you think.

[give card with alternatives to choose from:
Agree strongly
Agree
No particular opinion
Disagree

Disagree strongly]
[Read through the alternative answers]

C1 There are some mysteries in life that science will never explain.

There is a benevolent/good power behind the universe

The Churches have little importance these days.

Religion is something children have to make up their own minds about.

Religious education in school teaches us about right and wrong.

We ought to know about Christianity as part of our country's history.

It is important to go to Church or Sunday school.

It is important to have religious assemblies in school.

We should learn about different religions (ie.other than Christianity) at school.

Religious education is an important part of our education.

Now lastly I have some more general questions:
C2 Do you think there is a god? (if yes- what do you think god is?)

C3 Why do you think people go to Church

C4 What do people do in Church ?

C5 What does the Vicar do?

Bibliography

Ahern, G. and Davie, G. (1987), *Inner City God,* Hodder and Stroughton: London

Association of Religious Education Advisors and Inspectors, (July 1989), *Religious Education for ages 5 to 16-17 Attainment and Assessment Interim Consultative Report*

Baker, G.D. (1944), *Religious Education and the Education Act,* National Society: London

Bailey, E. (1985), *Civil Religion in Britain* Network for the Study of Implicit Religion, Winterbourne Rectory: Bristol.

Bailey, E. (ed.), (1986), *A Workbook in Popular Religion,* Partners Publications: Dorchester, Dorset

Bath Education Authority, (October 1970), *Revision of Agreed syllabus for Religious Education*

Bennett, S.N. et al., (1976), *Teaching Styles and Pupil Progress,* Open Books: London

Birmingham Education Committee, (1975), *Living Together. A Teachers' Handbook of Suggestions for Religious Education* City of Birmingham Education Committee

Blackburn Diocesan Board of Education, (1994), *Religious Education Syllabus for Church Schools,* Blackburn Diocesan Board of Education: North Lancashire Methodist District

Bocock, R. and Thompson, K. (eds), (1985), *Religion and Ideology,* Manchester University Press: Manchester

Brierley, P. (1991a), *'Christian' England,* Marc Europe: London

Brierley, P. (ed), (1991b), *Prospects for the Nineties South West. Trends and Tables from the English Church Census,* MARC Europe: London

Brierley, P. and Longley, D., (1991), *UK Christian Handbook (1992/93)* (ed), MARC Europe: London

British Journal of Religious Education, (Autumn 1978 - Summer 1992), Christian Education Movement: Derby

Burn, J. and Hart, C. (1988), *The Crisis in Religious Education,* The Educational Research Trust: London

Cambridgeshire Syllabus of Religious Teaching for Schools, (1951), Cambridge University Press: Cambridge

Catholic Herald, (19 February 1988), (15 April 1988)

Central Advisory Council for Education, (1967), *Children and their Primary School,* H.M.S.O.: London

Christian Education Movement, (c.1989), *What's the Use of RE?,* Derby: England

Church of England Yearbook, (1987 - 1991), Church House Publishing: London

Church Times, (1988-1996)

Copley, T. Priestley, J. Wadman, D. Coddington, V. (1990), *A FARE deal for R.E.: The Interim Report of the FARE project,* Exeter University School of Education: Exeter

Copley, T. Priestley, J. Wadman, D. Coddington, V. (1991), *Forms of Assessment in Religious Education The main report of the FARE project,* The FARE project, University of Exeter: Exeter

Cornwall Education Committee, (1936), *Syllabus of Religious Education*

Cornwall Education Committee, (1944), *Supplement to the Cornwall Syllabus of Religious Education*

Cornwall Education Committee, (1964), *Agreed Syllabus of Religious Education,* Darton Longman and Todd: London

Cornwall Education Committee (1971), *Handbook for Religious Education*

Cornwall County Council Education Committee, (1989), *Handbook of Religious Education*

Cornwall County Council Education Committee, (1989), *Syllabus for Religious Education in Cornwall*

Cornwall County Council. Education (1995) *Agreed Syllabus of Religious Education in Cornwall 1995-2000,* Cornwall County Council

Cornwall SACRE (1995) *Guidance on collective worship in county schools*

Cox, E. and Cairns, J.M. (1989), *Reforming Religious Education: The Religious Clauses of the 1988 Education Reform Act,* The Bedford Way Series, Institute of Education: University of London.

Davies, D. Pack, C. Seymour, S. Short, C. Watkins, C. and Winter, M. (1990), *Rural Church Project, The Views of Rural Parishioners*, Centre for Rural Studies: Royal Agricultural College, Cirencester and The Department of Theology: University of Nottingham, Vol. 4

Davie, G. (1990), Believing without Belonging: Is this the future of Religion in Britain?, *Social Compass,* Vol. 37, No. 4, 455 - 469

Department of Education and Science, (1989a), *National Curriculum: From Policy to Practice*

Department of Education and Science, (1989b), *Religious Education and Worship,* (Circular 3/89)

Duncan, G. (1990), *The Church School,* The National Society, Church of England: London

Durham Report, (1970), *The Fourth R: the Report of the Commission on Religious Education in Schools,* National Society and S.P.C.K.: London.

Durkheim, E. (1915), *The Elementary Forms of the Religious Life,* Translated by Swain, J.W., George Allen and Unwin: London

Faith in the City The Report of the Archbishop of Canterbury's Commission on Urban Priority Areas, (1985), Church House Publishing: London

Faulkner, J.(ed.), *The Religious Influence in Contemporary Society,* Merill, Columbia: Ohio

Field, F. (1989), *Opting Out: An Opportunity for Church Schools,* Church in Danger Group: London

Francis, L.J. (1984a), Monitoring the Christian Development of the Child, *Family, School and Church in Religious Education,* Occasional Paper 2, Department of Christian Ethics and Practical Theology, University of Edinburgh: Edinburgh

Francis, L.J (1984b), *Teenagers and the Church A Profile of Church-going Youth in the 1980's,* Collins Liturgical Publications: London

Francis, L.J.(1984c), *Assessing the Partnership 1944-84,* Culham College Institute Paper No.5, Culham College Institute: Oxford

Francis, L.J (1985), *Rural Anglicanism a Future for Young Christians?,* Collins: London

Francis, L.J. (1986a), 'Denominational Schools and Pupil Attitude Towards Christianity', *British Educational Research Journal,* Vol. 12, No. 2

Francis, L.J. (1986b), *Partnership in Rural Education. Church schools and teacher attitudes,* Collins: London

Francis, L.J.(1987), *Religion in the primary school: Partnership between Church and State?,* Collins: London

Francis, L.J. and Thatcher, A. (eds.), (1990), *Christian Perspectives for Education,* Fowler Wright Books: Leominster

Francis, L.J., Gibson, H.M. and Lankshear, D.W., (1991), "The influence of Protestant Sunday schools on attitudes towards Christianity among 11 - 15 year olds in Scotland', *British Journal of Religious Education,* Vol. 14, No. 1 pp.35-42

Francis, L.J. and Lankshear, D.W. (c.1992), *Continuing in the Way Children, Young People and the Church,* The National Society: London

Gay, J.D. (1982), *The Debate about Church schools in the Oxford Diocese,* Culham College: Oxford

Gay, J.D. (1985), *The size of Anglican primary schools,* Culham College, Institute Occasional Paper, No. 7, Culham College: Oxford

Gay, J.D. (1988), *Opting Out Grant Maintained Primary Schools,* Culham College Institute, Occasional Paper No. 9, Culham College: Oxford

General Synod Church of England Board of Education, (1979), *The Camberwell Papers The Church in Education,* General Synod and National Society: London

General Synod of the Church of England Board of Education, (1984), *Schools and Multi-Cultural Education A Discussion Paper,* Memorandum 2/84

General Synod of the Church of England Board of Education, (1988), *Children in the Way,* National Society, Church House Publishing

Gill, R. (1993), *The Myth of the Empty Church,* S.P.C.K., London

Goldman, R.J. (1964), *Religious Thinking from Childhood to Adolescence,* Routledge and Kegan Paul: London

Goldman, R.J. (1965), *Readiness for Religion A Basis for Developmental Religious Education,* Routledge and Kegan Paul: London

Greeley, A. (1992), 'Religion in Britain, Ireland and the USA', in Jowell, R. Brook, L. Prior, G. and Taylor, B. (eds), *British Social Attitudes, the 9th Report,* Dartmouth Publishing: Aldershot, England, pp.51-69.

Gretton, J. and Jackson, M. (1976), *William Tyndale: collapse of a school or a system?,* Allen and Unwin: London

Grimmitt, M. (1987), *Religious Education and Human Development,* McCrimmons Publishing Company: Great Wakering, Essex

Gripaios, P.(ed.), (1988), *The South West Economy 2,* Plymouth Business School: Plymouth

Groome, T.H. (1980), *Christian Religious Education,* Harper and Row: San Francisco

Habgood, J. (1983), *Church and Nation in a Secular Age,* Darton, Longman and Todd: London

Hammond, P.E. (ed.), (1985), *The Sacred in a Secular Age,* University of California Press: California

Hansard, Official Report Parliamentary Debates, H.M.S.O.: London

Hare Duke, M. and Whitton, E. (1977), *A Kind of Believing,* General Synod Board of Education, Church Information Office: London

Harrison, J. (1983), *Attitudes to Bible God and Church,* Bible Society: London

Havinden, M.A., Queniart, J. and Stanyer, J. (eds), (1991), *Centre and Periphery Brittany and Cornwall compared,* University of Exeter Press: Exeter

Hay, D. (1987), *Exploring Inner Space,* Mowbray: Oxford

Herberg, W. (1955), *Protestant Catholic Jew,* Country Life Press: Garden City, New York

H.M.S.O. (1990), *The Public General Acts and General Synod Measures 1988,* H.M.S.O.: London

Hoggart, R. (1957), *The Uses of Literacy,* Penquin: Harmondsworth, Middlesex

166

Holm, J. (1975), *Teaching Religion in School*, Oxford University Press: Oxford

Howard, W. and Mercier, C. (eds), (1990), *Religious Heritage and Personal Quest: Principles into Practice - The Berkshire Handbook:* Berkshire County Council

Howarth, R. (1993), 'The Impact of the Education Reform Act on New Agreed Syllabuses of Religious Education', *British Journal of Religious Education*, Vol.13, No.3, pp.162-167

Hull, J.M. (1985), *What Prevents Christian Adults from Learning?*, S.C.M. Press: London

Hull, J.M. (1989), *The Act Unpacked The Meaning of the 1988 Education Reform Act for Religious Education*, Birmingham papers in Religious Education, No.1., The University of Birmingham and the Christian Education Movement

Hull, J.M. (1994), 'Religious Education - a story of under-provision', *British Journal of Religious Education*, Vol.16, No. 3, pp.130-132

Hyde, K.E. (1990), *Religion in childhood and adolescence: a comprehensive review of the research*, Religious Education Press: Alabama

Inner London Education Authority (1968), *Learning for Life*, I.L.E.A.

Kay, B.W. (1988), *Managing the Church Schools A Study of the Governing Bodies of Church of England Aided Schools in the Oxford Diocese*, Occasional Paper No. 10, Culham College Institute: Oxford

Kay, W. (1981), *Religious thinking,attitudes and personality amongst secondary pupils in England and Ireland*, Unpub. D.Phil. thesis, University of Reading

Krarup, H. (1983), *Conventional Religion and Common Religion in Leeds Interview Schedule: Basic frequencies by question*, Religious Research, Papers 12, Department of Sociology,University of Leeds

Kumar, K. (1978), *Prophecy and Progress*, Penquin Books: Harmondsworth

Lankshear, D.W. (1992), *Governing Church Schools*, National Society: London

Leeds University, (1980-83), *Conventional Religion and Common Religion in Leeds*, Religious Research Papers, Department of Sociology, University of Leeds: Leeds

Learning for Living (1977-1978), Christian Education Movement: London

Lenski, G. (1961), *The Religious Factor*, Doubleday: USA

Leonard, M. (1988), *The 1988 Education Act A Tactical Guide for Schools*, Basil Blackwell: Oxford

Levitt, M. (1995a), 'The Church is very important to me'. A consideration of the relevance of Francis's 'Attitudes towards Christianity scale' to the aims of Church of England aided schools, *British Journal of Religious Education*, Vol. 17, no. 2, pp. 100-107

Levitt, M. (1995b), 'Sexual identity and religious socialization' *British Journal of Sociology,* Vol. 46, no. 3, pp. 529 - 536

London Diocesan Boards for Schools, (1988), *Religious Education in the Diocese of London Guidelines for Church Schools*

Loukes, H. (1961), *Teenage Religion* S.C.M. Press: London

Luckmann, T. (1967), *Invisible Religion,* Macmillan: New York

MacIntyre, A. (1981) *After Virtue a study in moral virtue,* Duckworth: London

Madge, V. (1965), *Children in search of meaning,* S.C.M. Press: London

Manchester Diocesan Council for Education, (1983), *Guidelines for Religious Education in Church primary schools*

Mann, H. (1853), *Census of Gt Britain 1851 Religious Worship England and Wales Report and Tables,* H.M.S.O.: London

Martin, D. (1967), *A Sociology of English Religion,* Heinemann: London

Martin, D. (1978), *A General Theory of Secularization,* Basil Blackwell: Oxford

McKrone, D., Kendrick, S and Straw, P. (eds), (1989), *The Making of Scotland: Nation, Culture and Social Change,* Edinburgh University Press: BSA, Edinburgh

Meakin, D.C. (1988) 'The Justification for Religious Education Reconsidered', *British Journal of Religious Education,* Vol. 10, No. 2, pp. 92-96

Moberly, W. (1942), *The Churches and the Teachers,* National Society/Press and Publications Board of the Church Assembly

National Curriculum Council, (1991), *Religious Education A Local Curriculum Framework,* N.C.C.: York, England

National Curriculum Council, (1993), *Spiritual and Moral Development - A Discussion Paper,* N.C.C.: York, England

National Society, (1839), *Terms of Union adopted by the General Committee of the National Society, (*19 February 1839), Appendix No 7, National Society: London

National Society, (1984), *A Future in Partnership,* National Society: London

National Society, (1985), *Positive Partnership,* National Society: Church of England for Promoting Religious Education, (GS 686), National Society: London

National Sociey, (1988), *Grant-Maintained Status and the Church School,* National Society: London

National Society, (1989a), *Religious Education,* National Society (Church of England) for Promoting Religious Education. London

National Society, (1989b), *School Worship,* National Society: London

National Society, (1990), *Terms of Union with the National Society,* Doc. BLT 005/24/4/90, National Society: London

National Society, (1991), *How Faith Grows,* National Society and Church House Publishing: London

Neal, D. (ed.), (1982), *Spirituality Across the Curriculum,* College of St.Mark and St. John Foundation: Plymouth

O'Keefe, B. (1986), *Faith, Culture and the Dual System,* Falmer Press East: Sussex

Orme, N (ed.), (1991), *Unity and Variety A History of the Church in Devon and Cornwall,* University of Exeter Press: Exter

Parsons, T. (1960), *Structure and Process in Modern Society,* Free Press: USA

Plymouth Business School, (1992-1995), *South West. The Economic Review,* Plymouth Business School, University of Plymouth: Plymouth

Plymouth Diocesan Year Book, (1989), Plymouth Diocese

Poyntz, C. and Walford, G. (1994), 'The New Christian Schools: a survey', *Educational Studies,* Vol.20, no.1, pp.127-143

Probert, J.C.C. (1971), *The Sociology of Cornish Methodism to the present day,* Cornish Methodist Historical Association

Religious Education Council, (1989), *Handbook for Agreed Syllabus Conferences, SACRE's and Schools*

Religious Education Council, (1984), *Religious Education Provision for England and Wales*

R.E. Today Magazine, 1988-96, Christian Education Movement Publications: Derby

Rhymer, J. (1983), *Religious Attitudes of Roman Catholic Secondary School Pupils in Strathclyde Region,* Unpublished PhD thesis, University of Edinburgh: Edinburgh

Robertson, R. (ed.), (1969), *Sociology of Religion,* Penguin: Harmondsworth

Robinson, E. and Jackson, M. (1987), *Religion and Values at Sixteen Plus,* Alister Hardy Research Centre, Christian Education Movement

Robinson, J.A.T. (1963), *Honest to God* S.C.M. Press: London

Robinson, J.A.T. and Edwards D.L. (1963), *The Honest to God Debate,* S.C.M. Press: London

Roof, W.C. and Gesch, L. 'Boomers and the culture of choice', in Ammerman, N.T. and Roof, W.C (eds), (1995), *Work, family and religion in contemporary society,* Routledge: New York, pp.61-79.

Runcie, R. (1982), *Address to the National Society,* National Society: London

Salisbury Diocesan Board of Education (ed.), *RE in the Church Aided Primary School Reviewing the Syllabus*

S.A.S.P.A.C. Census, (1981), *Small Area Statistics Cornwall and Isles of Scilly*

Schools Council, (1971), *Working Paper 36 Religious Education in Secondary Schools,* Evans and Methuen Educational: London

Schools Council, (1977), *Discovering an Approach,* Macmillan Education: London

Sheffield Diocese (1985), *A Handbook of suggestions for church schools*

Simon, B. and Gatton, M.J. (1975), *Observational Research and Classroom Learning Evaluation an S.S.R.C. Programme,* University of Leicester: Leicester

Smart, N. (1971), *The Religious Experience of Mankind,* Fontana Press: Glasgow

Smart, N. (1973), *The Phenomena of Religion,* Mowbray: Oxford

Social and Community Planning Research, (1992), *Cumulative Sourcebook: the first six surveys,* Gower Publishing: Aldershot, England.

Southern Examining Board, (Spring 1986), *Religious Studies Syllabus*

Sutcliffe, J. (ed.), (1984), *A Dictionary of Religious Education,* S.C.M. Press: London

Swann Report, (1985), *Education for All,* H.M.S.O.: London

Thomas, T. (ed.), *The British Their Religious Beliefs and Practices 1800-1986,* Routledge and Kegan Paul: London

Thompson, D.M. (1967), The Religious Census Problems and Possibilities. *Victorian Studies.* Vol.X1, No. 1, pp.87-97

Tilby, A. (1979), *Teaching God,* Fount: Glasgow

Toon, R. (1981), *Methodological Problems in the Study of Implicit Religion,* Religious Research Paper No. 3, Department. of Sociology, University of Leeds: Leeds

Tribe, D. (1970), *The Cost of Church Schools,* National Secular Society: London

Truro Diocese, (1988), *Church of England Aided Schools in the Diocese of Truro A Report on Worship and Religious Education in Church School*

Truro Diocese, Board of Education, (c. 1990), *Truro Diocesan Supplement to the Cornwall County Council Handbook of Religious Education*

Truro Diocese, (c. 1995), *Baptism and Communion*

Weber, M (1963), *The Sociology of Religion,* translated by Fischoff, Ephraim, Beacon Press

West Riding of Yorkshire Education Department, (1966), *Suggestions for Religious Education*

White, D. (1988), *Battered Bride?,* Monarch Publications: Eastborne, East Sussex

Wilson, B. (1982), *Religion in Sociological Perspective,* Oxford University Press

Wiltshire County Council Education Committee, (1967), *Religious Education in Wiltshire*

Yates, J. (1986), *Faith for the Future A Handbook of suggestions for Church schools,* National Society: London

Young, D. (1995, Learning to live in a world without maps, *Church Times* 6.10.95, p.14

DATE DUE

DEC 3	1 2004		